Fodor's 92
Pocket New York City

Theodore Fischer

Fodor's Travel Publications, Inc.
New York and London

ISBN 0-679-02079-9

Fodor's Pocket New York City

Editor: Paula Rackow
Contributors: Laura Broadwell, Suzanne Brown, Karen Cure, Jane Hershey, Penelope Papailias, Linda K. Schmidt, Craig Seligman
Art Director: Fabrizio La Rocca
Cartographer: David Lindroth
Illustrator: Karl Tanner
Cover Photograph: Owen Franken
Design: Vignelli Associates

Special Sales

Fodor's Travel Publications are available at special discounts for bulk purchases (100 copies or more) for sales promotions or premiums. Special editions, including personalized covers, excerpts of existing guides, and corporate imprints, can be created in large quantities for special needs. For more information write to Special Marketing, Fodor's Travel Publications, 201 East 50th Street, New York, NY 10022; or call 800/800-3246. Inquiries from the United Kingdom should be sent to Fodor's Travel Publications, 20 Vauxhall Bridge Rd., London, England SW1V 2SA.

MANUFACTURED IN
THE UNITED STATES OF AMERICA
10 9 8 7 6 5 4 3 2 1

Contents

Maps

Foreword

The sheer number of attractions and activities that New York City offers its guests can stagger both the first-time visitor and the experienced traveler. *Fodor's Pocket New York City* is intended especially for the new or short-term visitor who wants a complete but concise account of the most exciting places to see and the most interesting things to do.

Those who plan to spend more time in New York, or seek additional information about areas of interest, will want to consult *Fodor's New York City* for in-depth coverage of the city and her environs.

While every care has been taken to assure the accuracy of the information in this guide, the passage of time will always bring change, and consequently the publisher cannot accept responsibility for errors that may occur.

All prices and opening times quoted here are based on information supplied to us at press time. Hours and admission fees may change, however, and the prudent traveler will avoid inconvenience by calling ahead.

Fodor's wants to hear about your travel experiences, both pleasant and unpleasant. When a hotel or restaurant fails to live up to its billing, let us know and we will investigate the complaint and revise our entries where the facts warrant it.

Send your letters to the editors of Fodor's Travel Publications, 201 East 50th Street, New York, NY 10022.

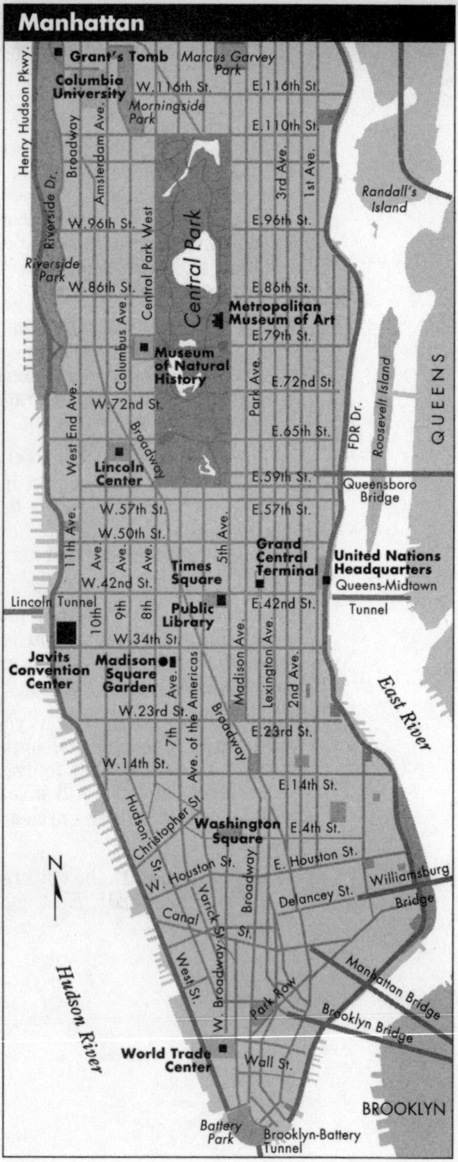
Manhattan
Grant's Tomb
Marcus Garvey Park
Columbia University
W. 116th St.
E. 116th St.
Morningside Park
E. 110th St.
Henry Hudson Pkwy.
Broadway
Amsterdam Ave.
3rd Ave.
1st Ave.
Randall's Island
Riverside Dr.
W. 96th St.
E. 96th St.
Central Park West
Central Park
Riverside Park
W. 86th St.
E. 86th St.
Metropolitan Museum of Art
Columbus Ave.
E. 79th St.
Museum of Natural History
Park Ave.
E. 72nd St.
Roosevelt Island
QUEENS
West End Ave.
W. 72nd St.
Broadway
E. 65th St.
FDR Dr.
Lincoln Center
E. 59th St.
Queensboro Bridge
W. 57th St.
E. 57th St.
11th Ave.
W. 50th St.
5th Ave.
Grand Central Terminal
United Nations Headquarters
Ave.
Ave.
Ave.
Times Square
W. 42nd St.
Queens-Midtown Tunnel
Lincoln Tunnel
10th
9th
8th
Public Library
E. 42nd St.
W. 34th St.
Madison Ave.
Lexington Ave.
2nd Ave.
Javits Convention Center
Madison Square Garden
Ave.
Ave. of the Americas
East River
W. 23rd St.
Broadway
E. 23rd St.
7th
W. 14th St.
E. 14th St.
Hudson St.
Christopher St.
Washington Square
E. 4th St.
E. Houston St.
N
W. Houston St.
Williamsburg Bridge
Varick St.
Broadway
Delancey St.
Canal St.
West St.
W. Broadway
Manhattan Bridge
Hudson River
Park Row
Brooklyn Bridge
World Trade Center
Wall St.
BROOKLYN
Battery Park
Brooklyn-Battery Tunnel

Manhattan Neighborhoods

Manhattan Subways

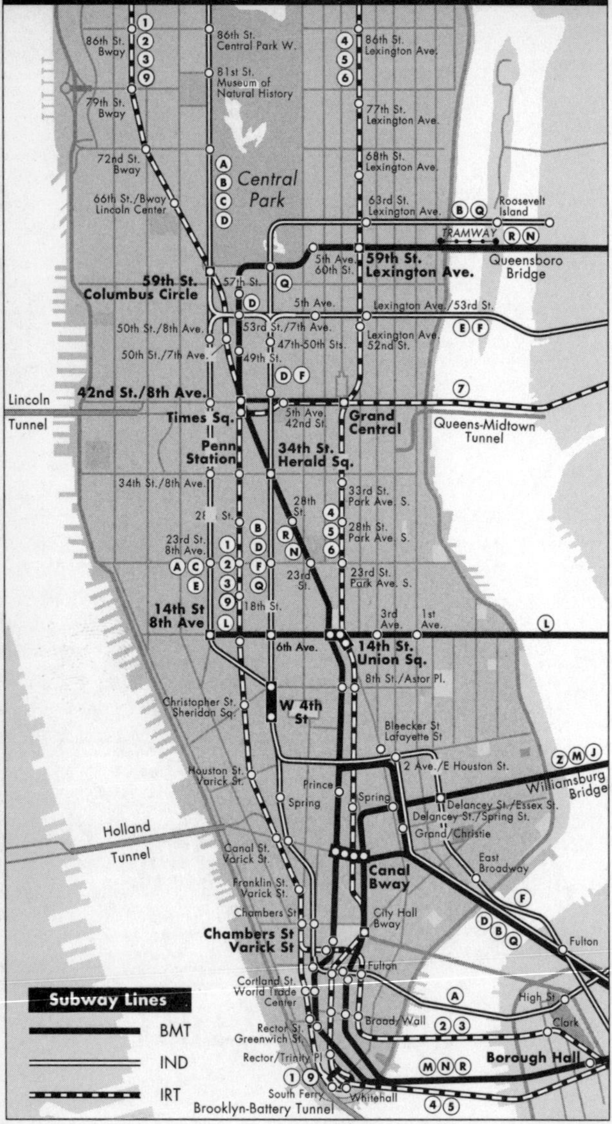

Introduction

Whatever you're looking for in a big-city vacation, you'll find in New York.

The city has history: You can trace the life of the early Dutch settlers, canny traders who, unconstrained by religious strictures of fellow colonists in Massachusetts and Pennsylvania, gave the city its enterprising soul. You can see the spot where George Washington was sworn in as first U.S. president, the grave of Alexander Hamilton, and the restored site of America's greatest 19th-century seaport.

The city has architecture: "New York" and "skyline" are virtually a single word. But along with a succession of buildings that, in their time, ranked as the world's tallest structures (the Flatiron, Woolworth, Chrysler, and Empire State buildings, and the World Trade Center Towers), New York retains many handsome residential reminders of its Colonial and Victorian past. Contemporary architectural treasures range from the bizarre (Guggenheim Museum) to the sublime (Trump Tower) to the perplexingly postmodern (AT&T Building).

No one has to make a case for New York's performing arts. In show-biz terms, the Big Apple is top banana. A New York street by the name of Broadway is an international adjective for theater. The Metropolitan Opera, New York Philharmonic, and New York City Ballet are national companies. Their greatness is nurtured by the talent of hundreds of non-Broadway theaters, musical ensembles, and dance troupes—all performing nightly in New York. The city remains the world center of jazz, rock, and dance music attuned to every generation.

New York has a full complement of professional sports organizations: two baseball teams (Mets and Yankees), two football teams (Giants and Jets), two basketball teams (Knicks and New Jersey Nets), and three hockey teams (Rangers, Islanders, New Jersey Devils). It's easy to find a boxing or wrestling match. And horse races, both thoroughbred and standardbred, are off and running almost every day of the year at one of the four area tracks.

Perhaps because New York lacks the outdoor endowments of other locales, the city places a stronger emphasis on the joys of the table. New York has 17,000 restaurants, some world-famous institutions, others the "in" spots of the day, neighborhood standbys, or back-street discoveries.

Even though the island of Manhattan has largely become a river-to-river high-rent district, its ethnic neighborhoods thrive. Little Italy, Chinatown, and other pockets of ethnicity are not theme parks but vibrant, ever-changing areas that remain magnets for Old Country settlers.

Some New York attractions occupy a class by themselves. The Statue of Liberty, the Brooklyn Bridge, the Empire State Building, Times Square, and Central Park may be situated in New York City, but all belong to the world.

Above and beyond the laundry list of sights and activities, New York has an undefinable aura that exists nowhere else. It's a kind of energy level that has something to do with being in the big league, where everybody's watching and keeping score.

Part of the big-league mentality derives from the kind of industries headquartered here. New York has Wall Street, the financial center of the world. It contains the corporate headquarters of major TV networks, most national magazines, book publishers, and news-gathering organizations. The largest advertising agencies and public relations firms are here. New York also has the fashion industry and the United Nations. A lot goes on here, and a lot of people are around to tell about it.

Walking down a New York street, you might pass Henry Kissinger (with a bodyguard or two). You could go into a restaurant and get a table across from Robert DeNiro. You are very likely to turn a corner and see a feature film or TV series being filmed. And even if you don't see someone you recognize, you always feel that you just *might*. Paraphrasing a slogan coined for The Plaza hotel, you get the feeling that "nothing unimportant ever happens in New York," and it lends an edge to everything that goes on.

You may already have heard that New York can be an expensive place in which to live or to visit. New York hotels are among the country's most costly, and the price ranges of Manhattan restaurants seem to be a couple of levels above those one finds elsewhere in the country. Movie tickets, museum admissions, clothing, drinks, incidentals—many things cost more here. Yet there are shopping bargains in New York; those things that New York produces, such as books, can often be found at much lower prices here than in the other 49 states.

And there is crime, which can occur in the most unexpected places. The person who appears to have an accident at the exit door of a bus is in reality a pickpocket who will flee with your wallet or purse if you attempt to give aid. The individual who approaches you with a complicated story about having "found" money or other valuables is playing a confidence game and hopes to get something from you. Violent crime can occur anywhere, at any hour, and the only reasonable precautions anyone can take are to keep jewelry and valuables out of sight on the street and to walk generally on the main thoroughfares, with the crowds. Women should never hang a purse on a chair in a restaurant or on a hook in a rest room stall.

New Yorkers themselves often appear to be haughty, cold, even rude in their manner. This is largely a defensive attitude that residents develop, consciously or not, to cope with living so closely with so many other people. When you encounter rudeness, don't take it personally; it's just that individual's way of behaving. And when you have the opportunity to talk for a bit with New Yorkers, you'll find that they usually warm to you and will often go out of their way to be accommodating.

Many are the tales of visitors lost on the subway who are shepherded to safety by a Good Samaritan from Canarsie. Strangers constantly come forward to mediate disputes between out-of-towners and cab drivers. Ask New Yorkers for simple directions and they're likely to tell you a lot more than you need to know. New Yorkers can be as down-to-earth as people anywhere. Yet they can also be brash, opinionated, impatient, smug, self-important, and, in a peculiar way, maddeningly provincial. As O. Henry wrote, "What else can you expect from a town that's shut off from the world by the ocean on one side and New Jersey on the other?"

America's greatest metropolis presents the visitor with a superfluity of opportunity. You can't do it all; you don't have the time, and nobody has the money. So you will have to make decisions, and the big one will probably be whether you see what New York does best or you do the things that you like best. On the whole, that's a great choice to have.

1 Essential Information

Before You Go

Visitor Information

In North America. Contact **The New York Convention and Visitors Bureau** (2 Columbus Circle, New York, NY 10019, tel. 212/397–8222) and the **New York Division of Tourism** (1 Commerce Plaza, Albany, NY 12245, tel. 800/225–5697 or 518/474–4116). Ask for the *I Love New York* series of booklets.

Tips for British Travelers

Passports and Visas You will need a valid passport (cost £15). You do not need a visa if you are staying for fewer than 90 days and have a return ticket with a major airline. There are some exceptions to this, so check with your travel agent or with the United States Embassy (Visa and Immigration Dept., 5 Upper Grosvenor St., London W1A 2JB, tel. 071/499–3443). No vaccinations are required.

Customs Entering the United States, you may bring 200 cigarettes, 50 cigars or 2 kilograms of tobacco; 1 liter of alcohol; duty-free gifts to a value of $100. Be careful not to take in meat or meat products, seeds, plants, fruits, etc. Avoid illegal drugs like the plague.

Returning to Britain you may bring home, if you are 17 or older: (1) 200 cigarettes or 100 cigarillos or 50 cigars or 250 grams of tobacco; (2) two liters of table wine with additional allowances for (a) one liter of alcohol over 22% by volume (38.8° proof, most spirits), (b) two liters of alcohol under 22% by volume, or (c) two more liters of table wine; and (3) 60 milliliters of perfume and 250 milliliters of toilet water, and (4) other goods up to a value of £32, but no more than 50 liters of beer or 25 lighters.

Insurance We recommend that you insure yourself to cover health and motoring mishaps. **Europ Assistance** (252 High St., Croydon, Surrey CR0 1NF, tel. 081/680–1234).

It is also wise to take out insurance to cover loss of luggage (though check that this isn't already covered in an existing homeowner's policy). Trip-cancellation insurance is another wise buy.

The Association of British Insurers (Aldermary House, 10–15 Queen St., London EC4N 1TT, tel. 081/248–4477) will give comprehensive advice on all aspects of vacation insurance.

Tour Operators Most tour operators now offer excellent budget packages to the U.S. Among those to consider are:

Albany Travel (Manchester) Ltd. (Central Buildings, 211 Deansgate, Manchester M2 5QR, tel. 061/833–0202).

American Airplan (Airplan House, Churchfield Rd., Walton-on-Thames, Surrey KT12 2TJ, tel. 0932/231422 for information, 0932/246347 for brochures).

American Travel Centre (77 Victoria St., Windsor, Berkshire SL4 1EH, tel. 0753/831300).

Jetsave (Sussex House, London Rd., East Grinstead, Sussex RH19 1LD, tel. 0342/312033).

Thomas Cook Ltd. (Box 36, Thorpe Wood, Peterborough PE3 6SB, tel. 0733/332333).

Speedbird Holidays (Pacific House, Hazelwick Ave., Crawley, W. Sussex RH10 1NP, tel. 0293/611611).

Airfares We suggest that you explore the current scene for budget flight possibilities. Unfortunately, there are few standby programs on any of the major airlines, but do check their APEX and other fares, which offer a considerable saving over the full price. Quite frankly, only some business travelers who don't have to watch the price of their tickets fly full-price these days—and find themselves sitting right beside an APEX passenger! At press time, a low-season APEX round-trip fare to New York costs £416 and up. The small daily and Sunday newspaper ads are also a good source of bargain price flights.

Information One excellent source of information is the **State of New York Division of Tourism** (2 Cinnamon Row, Plantation Wharf, York Place, London SW11 3TW, tel. 071/978–5275). Although they are not open for personal callers, they will be happy to send brochures and other information.

What to Pack

Pack light because porters and luggage trolleys are hard to find. Luggage allowances on domestic flights vary slightly from airline to airline. Most allow three checked pieces and one carry-on. Some give you the option of two checked pieces and two carry-ons. In general, check-in luggage may not weigh more than 70 pounds each or be larger than 62 inches (length + width + height). Carry-on luggage may not be larger than 45 inches (length + width + height) and must fit under the seat or in the overhead luggage compartment.

New York City has many restaurants that require men to wear a jacket and tie. For sightseeing and casual dining, jeans and sneakers are acceptable just about anywhere. Sneakers seem to be the universal walking shoe, especially among women, regardless of whether they are wearing business suits, shorts, or slacks. New York can be very cold in the winter, but there's not much snow. The humidity tends to be high in summer, so leave the plastic raincoats at home.

Cash Machines

Virtually all U.S. banks belong to a network of ATMs (Automatic Teller Machines), which dispense cash 24 hours a day in cities throughout the country. There are some eight major networks in the United States, the largest of which are Cirrus, owned by MasterCard, and Plus, affiliated with Visa. Some banks belong to more than one network. These cards are not automatically issued; you have to ask for them. Cards issued by Visa, MasterCard, and American Express may also be used in the ATMs, but the fees are usually higher than the fees on bank cards, and there is a daily interest charge on the "loan," even if monthly bills are paid on time. Each network has a toll-free number you can call to locate machines in a given city. The Cirrus number is 800/4–CIRRUS; the Plus number is 800/THE–PLUS. Check with your bank for fees and for the amount of cash you can withdraw on any given day.

Car Rentals

We cannot urge you strongly enough to avoid bringing a car into Manhattan. Street parking is extremely scarce (violators are towed away literally within minutes), garages cost as much as $15 for two hours in some neighborhoods, and daytime Manhattan gridlock can fray the calmest nerves.

That said, you may still need a car, perhaps for a weekend escape or because Manhattan is part of a longer trip. New York offers an unusually confusing array of car rental possibilities. The old ploy of renting out of Newark Airport to take advantage of lower rates no longer works. Prices charged by major national firms are the same at Newark, Kennedy, and LaGuardia airports, as well as at Manhattan rental locations. Expect to pay $50–$80 per day for a subcompact with unlimited mileage. Companies with multiple Manhattan and airport locations include: **Dollar** (tel. 800/800–4000), **Budget** (tel. 800/527–0700), **Thrifty** (tel. 800/367–2277), **National** (tel. 800/328–4567), **Hertz** (tel. 800/654–3131), and **Avis** (tel. 800/331–1212). Some regional budget companies like **Rent-A-Wreck** (tel. 800/221–8282) offer lower rates. If you are flying into LaGuardia or Kennedy, you might look into some local Queens agencies with lower rates, such as **ABC** (tel. 800/247–6110) or **Universal** (tel. 718/786–0786). **Sunshine Rent-A-Car** (tel. 212/989–7260) is good for budget rentals in Greenwich Village.

Whomever you rent from, get a reservation number and ask if there is free mileage and if you must pay for a full tank of gas whether you use it or not.

Arriving and Departing

By Plane

The Airlines Virtually every major U.S. and foreign airline serves one or more of New York's three airports: **LaGuardia Airport, John F. Kennedy Interna-**

tional Airport, and **Newark International Airport.**

When choosing a flight, be sure to distinguish among (a) *nonstop flights*—no stops or changes of aircraft; (b) *direct flights*—one or more stops but no change of aircraft; (c) *connecting flights*—at least one change of aircraft and possibly several stops as well.

Airlines serving the New York area include: America West (tel. 800/247–5692), American (tel. 800/433–7300), Continental (tel. 800/525–0280), Delta (tel. 800/221–1212), Midway (tel. 800/621–5700), Northwest (tel. 800/225–2525), Pan Am (tel. 800/442–5896), TWA (tel. 800/221–2000), United (tel. 800/241–6522), and USAir (tel. 800/428–4322).

Smoking is banned on all routes within the 48 contiguous states; within the states of Hawaii and Alaska; to and from the U.S. Virgin Islands and Puerto Rico; and on flights of under six hours to and from Hawaii and Alaska. The rule applies to the domestic legs of all foreign routes but does not apply to international flights.

On a flight where smoking is permitted, you can request a nonsmoking seat during check-in or when you book your ticket. If you are told that there are no seats available in the nonsmoking section on the day of the flight, insist on one: Department of Transportation regulations require carriers to find seats for all nonsmokers, provided they meet check-in time restrictions.

From Airports to Center City

LaGuardia Airport is in the borough of Queens, eight miles northeast of midtown Manhattan. Taxis cost $14–$20 plus toll (up to $2.50) and take 20–40 minutes. Group taxi rides to Manhattan are available at taxi dispatch lines just outside the baggage-claim areas during most travel hours (no service Saturdays or holidays). Group fares range from $8 to $9 per person (plus share of tolls), depending on your destination. Call 718/784–4343 for more information.

Carey Airport Express (tel. 718/632–0500) buses depart for Manhattan every 20 minutes from 5:30 AM–1 AM (weekends 6 AM–1 AM) It's a 20–30 minute ride to 42nd Street and Park Avenue, directly opposite Grand Central Terminal. The bus continues from here to the Port Authority Bus Terminal, the New York Hilton, Sheraton City Squire, Crown Plaza Holiday Inn, and Marriott Marquis hotels. To other midtown hotels, it's a short cab ride. The bus fare is $7.50; pay the driver. The **Gray Line Air Shuttle Minibus** (tel. 212/ 757–6840) serves major Manhattan hotels direct to and from the airport. The fare is $11 per person; make arrangements at the ground transportation center or use the courtesy phone.

John F. Kennedy International Airport (JFK) is in the borough of Queens, 15 miles southeast of midtown. Taxis cost $24–$30 plus tolls (up to $2.50) and take 35–60 minutes.

Carey Airport Express (tel. 718/632–0500) buses depart for Manhattan from all JFK terminals every 30 minutes from 5 AM–1 AM. The ride takes about one hour to 42nd Street and Park Avenue (Grand Central Terminal). The bus continues from there to the New York Hilton, Sheraton City Squire, and Marriott Marquis hotels; it's a short cab ride to other midtown hotels. The bus fare is $9.50; pay the driver. The **Gray Line Air Shuttle Minibus** (tel. 212/ 757–6840) serves major Manhattan hotels directly from the airport; the cost is $14 per person. Make arrangements at the ground transportation counter or use the courtesy phone.

Newark International Airport is in Newark, New Jersey, 16 miles southwest of Midtown. Taxis cost $28–$30 plus tolls ($3) and take 20–45 minutes. "Share and Save" group rates are available for up to four passengers between 8 AM and midnight; make arrangements with the taxi dispatcher.

NJ Transit Airport Express buses (tel. 201/460–8444) depart every 15–30 minutes for the Port Authority Terminal, at 42nd Street and Eighth Avenue. From there it's a short cab ride to midtown hotels. The ride takes 30–45 minutes. The fare is $7; buy your ticket inside the terminal.

The **Olympia Airport Express Bus** (tel. 212/964–6233) to the World Trade Center and Grand Central Terminal departs every 20 minutes from 6:15 AM to midnight. The travel time to the World Trade Center is 20 minutes; to Grand

Central, 35 minutes. The fare is $7; pay the driver.

The Gray Line Air Shuttle Minibus (tel. 212/757-6840) serves major Manhattan hotels directly to and from the airport. You pay $16 per passenger; make arrangements at the airport's ground transportation center or use the courtesy phone.

By Car

The **Lincoln Tunnel** (I–495), **Holland Tunnel,** and **George Washington Bridge** (I–95) connect to the New Jersey Turnpike system and points west. The Lincoln Tunnel leads to midtown Manhattan, the Holland Tunnel to lower Manhattan, the George Washington Bridge to northern Manhattan. Each of the three arteries requires a toll ($4 for cars) eastbound into New York, but no toll westbound.

From Long Island, the **Midtown Tunnel** (I–495) and **Triborough Bridge** (I–278) are the most direct arteries to Manhattan. Both require tolls ($2.50 for cars) in both directions.

From upstate New York, the city is accessible via the **New York (Dewey) Thruway** (I–87) (toll) and the **Major Deegan Expressway** (I–87) through the Bronx and across the **Triborough Bridge** (toll).

From New England, the **Connecticut Turnpike** (I–95) connects to the **New England Thruway** (I–95) (toll), the **Bruckner Expressway** (I–278), and the **Triborough Bridge** (toll) to upper Manhattan.

Be forewarned: The deterioration of city bridges is a serious problem, and repairs will be ongoing for the next few years. Don't be surprised if a bridge is partially or completely closed.

Driving within Manhattan can be a nightmare of gridlocked streets and predatory fellow motorists. Free parking is almost impossible to find in Midtown, and parking lots are exorbitant—$16 for three hours is not unusual in midtown lots—all over town. If you do drive, don't plan to use your car much for driving within Manhattan.

By Train

Amtrak (tel. 800/872–7245) offers frequent service within the Northeast Corridor, between Boston and Washington. Trains arrive and de part from Pennsylvania Station (31st to 33rd Sts., between Seventh and Eighth Aves.). Amtrak service from Montreal and upstate New York and the Lake Shore Limited from Chicago also use Penn Station, as do trains from the Southeast, Midwest, and Far West.

Metro-North Commuter Railroad (tel. 212/532–4900) serves Grand Central from the northern suburbs and Connecticut as far east as New Haven. The **Long Island Railroad** (tel. 718/217–5477) has service from all over Long Island to Penn Station. Also at Penn Station, **New Jersey Transit** (tel. 201/460–8444) offers frequent service from the north and central regions of the state.

By Bus

All long-haul and commuter bus lines feed into the **Port Authority Terminal,** a mammoth multilevel structure that occupies a nearly two-square-block area between 40th and 42nd streets and Eighth and Ninth avenues. Though it's recently modernized and fairly clean, the large number of vagrants make the terminal an uncomfortable place to spend much time. Especially on night arrivals, plan to move swiftly through the terminal.

For information on any service into or out of the Port Authority Terminal, call 212/564–8484. Some of the individual bus lines serving New York include **Greyhound-Trailways** (consult local information for a number in your area), **Adirondack** and **Pine Hill Trailways** from upstate New York (tel. 914/339–4230 or 212/947–5300); **Bonanza Bus Lines** from New England (tel. 800/556–3815); **Martz Trailways** from northeastern Pennsylvania (tel. 800/233–8604); **Peter Pan Bus Lines** from New England (tel. 413/781–2900); and **Vermont Transit** from New England (tel. 802/862–9671).

Staying in New York City

Important Addresses and Numbers

Tourist Information The **New York Convention and Visitors Bureau** at Columbus Circle (58th St. and Eighth Ave.) provides a wealth of free information, including brochures, subway and bus maps, listings of hotels and weekend hotel packages, and discount coupons for Broadway shows. Drop in or, better yet, contact them before you arrive. *2 Columbus Circle, New York, NY 10019, tel. 212/397–8222. Open weekdays 9–6, weekends 10–6. Closed holidays.*

Emergencies 911 for **police, fire,** or **ambulance** in an emergency.

Doctor **Doctors On Call, 24-hour house-call service** at 212/737–2333. Near Midtown, 24-hour emergency rooms are open at **St. Luke's–Roosevelt Hospital** (58th St. at 9th Ave., tel. 212/523–6800) and **St. Vincent's Hospital** (Seventh Ave. at 11th St., tel. 212/790–7997).

Dentist The **Dental Emergency Service** (212/679–3966; after 8 PM, tel. 212/679–4172) will make a referral.

24-hour Pharmacy **Kaufman's Pharmacy** (Lexington Ave. at 50th St., tel. 212/755–2266).

Getting Around

New York is a city of neighborhoods best explored at a leisurely pace, up close, and by foot. But New York neighborhoods are big, and you'll need some motorized means of travel between them.

By Subway The 244-mile subway system is the fastest and cheapest way to get around the city. It operates 24 hours a day and, especially within Manhattan, serves most of the places you'll want to visit. The New York subway also deserves many of the negative aspects of its image. Even though new graffiti-proof, air-conditioned cars predominate now, many trains are crowded, dirty, noisy, somewhat unreliable, and occasionally unsafe. Unsavory characters lurk in the stations, and panhandlers, who are noisy but usually harmless, work their way through the cars. Don't write off the subway—it really is colorful, and millions ride it every day without incident—but stay alert at all times.

At press time the subway cost $1.15 (though an increase is expected), with reduced fares for the disabled and senior citizens at all hours. You must use a token to enter. They are sold at token booths that are *usually* open at each station. It's advisable to stock up on tokens since the booth may not be open and, if open, may have a long line. You can also use tokens on city buses. A token permits unlimited subway transfers.

Free subway maps are given out at token booths upon request. They are often out of stock, so ask at several booths until you find one. Maps are also posted in subway cars but are seldom found on platforms. Make sure you refer to an up-to-date map; lengthy repair programs often cause reroutings that last long enough for new "temporary" maps to be printed.

For route information, ask the token clerk or a transit policeman. And don't hesitate to ask directions from fellow riders: Once New Yorkers realize you're harmless, they bend over backward to help. Call 718/330–1234 for information from 6 AM to 9 PM daily. (Calls from the 212 area code to 718, and vice versa, cost the local rate, 25¢ from pay phones.)

A few words on safety: Most of the stops in Midtown are crowded with riders all hours of the day or night. Stay among those crowds—there's safety in numbers. Don't wander off to a deserted section of the platform, and don't enter empty or nearly empty cars. At off-peak hours, try to ride in the same car as the conductor; it will stop near a line of light bulbs above the edge of the platform. Follow the crowd until you reach the comparative safety of the street.

By Bus Most buses follow easy-to-understand routes along the Manhattan grid. Routes go up or down the north-south avenues, east and west on the major two-way crosstown streets. Most bus routes operate 24 hours, but service is infrequent late at night. Buses are great for sightseeing, but traffic jams—a potential threat at any time or place in Manhattan—can make rides maddeningly slow.

At press time bus fare was $1.15 (though an increase is expected) in change (no pennies; no change given) or a token. When you get on the bus you can get a free transfer good for one change to an intersecting route. Transfer points are listed on the back of the transfer. Transfers have time limits of at least two hours. You cannot use the transfer to enter the subway.

Each of the five boroughs of New York has a separate bus map, and they are scarcer than hen's teeth. They are occasionally available in subway token booths and never available on buses. Your best bets are the Convention and Visitors Bureau at Columbus Circle or the information kiosks in Grand Central Terminal and Penn Station.

By Taxi Taxis are usually easy to hail on the street or from a line in front of major hotels. Taxis cost $1.50 for the first ⅕ mile, 25¢ for each ⅕ mile thereafter, and 25¢ for each 75 seconds not in motion. A 50¢ surcharge is added to rides begun between 8 PM and 6 AM. There is no charge for extra passengers. Taxi drivers also expect a 15% tip. Barring performance above and beyond the call of duty, don't feel obliged to give them more.

To avoid unhappy taxi experiences, be sure to have a general idea of where you want to go. Some cab drivers are dishonest; some are ignorant; some can barely understand English. In any case, if you don't have any idea of the proper route, you may be taken for a long and costly ride.

New York taxis are mile-for-mile less expensive than in many places, and in some instances taxis can be a bargain. A short trip for two or more people may cost less than the combined bus or subway fare.

Jogging The principal area for jogging is Central Park, a runner's paradise from dawn till sundown. A 1.59 mile soft surface track rings the Reservoir (Fifth Ave. at 90th St.). For information on group runs, call the **Road Runners Club** (tel. 212/860–4455).

Bicycling You can rent bikes in Central Park from **AAA Bikes in Central Park,** located beside the Loeb Boathouse parallel to 72nd Street (tel. 212/861–4137). Outside but near the park, you can rent bikes from **Metro Bicycles** (1311 Lexington Ave. at 88th St., tel. 212/427–4450); **Bicycles Plus** (204 E. 85th St., tel. 212/794–2201), and **Gene's Bicycles** (242 E. 79th St., tel. 212/249–9218).

Guided Tours

Orientation Tours The most pleasant way to get a crash orientation to Manhattan is aboard a **Circle Line Cruise.** Once you've finished the three-hour, 35-mile circumnavigation of Manhattan, you'll have a good idea of where things are and what you want to see next. Narrations are as interesting and individualized as the guides—often moonlighting actors—who deliver them. *Pier 83, west end of 42nd St., tel. 212/563–3200. Fare: $15 adults, $7.50 children under 12. Operates early Mar.–Dec., Tues.–Sun.*

At South Street Seaport's Pier 16 you can take two- or three-hour voyages to New York's past aboard the iron cargo schooner, *Pioneer* (tel. 212/669–9416). You can take 90-minute tours of New York Harbor aboard the sidewheeler *Andrew Fletcher* or the re-created steamboat *DeWitt Clinton.*

For a shorter excursion, the **TNT Express,** a hydroliner, will show you the island of Manhattan in 75 minutes. *Pier 11, south of South Street Seaport, tel. 212/244–4770. Fare: $15 adults, $13 senior citizens, $8 children under 12, under 5 free. Boats depart Mon.–Sat. noon and 2 PM.*

Gray Line (900 Eighth Ave. at 53rd St., tel. 212/397–2600) offers a number of different city bus tours, plus cruises and day trips to Brooklyn and Atlantic City. **Short Line Tours** (166 W. 46th St., tel. 212/354–5122) offers some 20 different tour options.

Island Helicopter (Heliport at E. 34th St. and East River, tel. 212/683–4575) offers four flyover options, from $41 (for 7 miles) to $94 (for 34 miles). From the West Side, **Liberty** (heliport at W. 30th St. and Hudson River, tel. 212/465–8905) has three tours ranging from $55 to $99.

Special-interest Tours

Backstage on Broadway (tel. 212/575–8065) puts you in a Broadway theater setting and lets you mingle with show people. Reservations are mandatory. **Art Tours of Manhattan** (tel. 609/921–2647) provides an inside view of museum and gallery exhibits. **Gallery Passports** (tel. 212/288–3578) takes you to galleries and museums as well as artists' studios and lofts in Manhattan. **Soho Art Experience** (tel. 212/219–0810) offers tours of Soho's architecture, galleries, shops, and artists' lofts. **Doorway to Design** (tel. 212/221–1111) tours fashion and interior design showrooms as well as artists' private studios. **Harlem Your Way!** (tel. 212/690–1687) offers daily walking tours and Sunday gospel trips to one of the most exciting areas of the city.

Walking Tours

Sidewalks of New York (Box 1660, Cathedral Station, New York, NY 10025, tel. 212/517–0201) hits the streets from various thematic angles—Historic Church Tours, Ye Old Tavern Tours, Celebrity Home Tours, Final Resting Places of the Rich and Famous Tours. Tours are offered on weekends, both days and evenings, year-round. Tours last 2–2½ hours and cost $10; no reservations are required. **Adventure on a Shoestring** (300 W. 53rd St., New York, NY 10019, tel. 212/265–2663) is an organization dating from 1963 that explores unique New York neighborhoods. Tours are scheduled periodically, $5 per person. **The Municipal Art Society** (tel. 212/935–3960) operates a series of bus and walking tours. The **Urban Park Rangers** (tel. 212/427–4040) offers weekend walks and workshops, most of them free, in city parks. The **92nd Street Y** (tel. 212/996–1105) always has something special to offer on weekends.

The most comprehensive listing of tours offered during a particular week is published in the "Other Events" section of *New York* magazine's "Cue" listings.

Self-guided Walking Tours

The **New York Convention and Visitors Bureau** publishes an "I Love New York Visitors Guide," available at the bureau's information center (2 Columbus Circle, tel. 212/397–8222). Walkers in Brooklyn can pick up free maps at the public affairs desk of the Brooklyn Borough President's office (209 Joralemon St., 3rd floor). The same maps can be obtained by mail, at $5 each, from the Fund for the Borough of Brooklyn (16 Court St., Suite 1400 W., Brooklyn, NY 11241; tel. 718/855–7882).

The **Municipal Art Society of New York** has prepared a comprehensive "Juror's Guide to Lower Manhattan: Five Walking Tours" for the benefit of jurors who are often required to kill a lot of time while serving in downtown courthouses. Along with an explanation of the New York jury system, the pamphlet includes tours of Lower Manhattan and Wall Street; City Hall District; Chinatown and Little Italy; South Street Seaport; and TriBeCa. Jurors get copies free; nonjurors can purchase copies at Urban Center Books (457 Madison at 51st St., New York, NY 10022, tel. 212/935–3595).

A free "Walking Tour of Rockefeller Center" pamphlet is available from the information desk in the lobby of the GE Building (30 Rockefeller Plaza).

2 Exploring New York City

Orientation

Visitors finding their way their way around the city soon discover that Manhattan has a Jekyll-and-Hyde personality. Rational Dr. Jekyll dwells above 14th Street, where the streets form a regular grid pattern. Avenues run north (uptown) and south (downtown). Streets run east and west (crosstown). The exceptions are Broadway, a diagonal from 14th to 79th streets, and the thoroughfares along the Hudson and East rivers.

Fifth Avenue (originally Middle Road) is the baseline: Street addresses begin at Fifth Avenue and increase in regular increments. East of Fifth, the addresses 1–99 E. are between Fifth and Park avenues; 100–199 E. between Park and Third avenues; 200–299 E. between Third and Second avenues; and so on. West of Fifth Avenue, the addresses 1–99 W. are between Fifth and Sixth avenues; 100–199 W. between Sixth and Seventh avenues; 200–299 W. between Seventh and Eighth avenues; and so on. Above 59th Street, West Side addresses begin at Central Park West, an extension of Eighth Avenue.

Avenue addresses are much less regular. The building numbers begin wherever the avenue begins, and they increase by irregular increments. An address at 552 Third Avenue, for example, will not be at the same cross street as (or necessarily anywhere near) 552 Second Avenue or 552 Lexington Avenue. Avenue addresses given in this book (and in many other listings) include both the number and the nearest cross street, for example, "303 Lexington Avenue at 37th Street." When you don't know the nearest cross street, you can calculate the location of an avenue address by referring to the formulas in the Manhattan Address Locator (*see* below).

Below 14th Street, Manhattan streets reflect the disordered personality of Mr. Hyde. They are either diagonals aligned with present or long-gone shorelines or the twisting descendants of an ancient cow path. Below 14th Street you will encounter such anomalous situations as the intersection of West 4th Street and West 11th Street, the misunderstandings caused by

Manhattan Address Locator

To locate avenue addresses, take the address, cancel the last figure, divide by 2, add or subtract the key number below. The answer is the nearest numbered cross street, approximately. To find addresses on numbered cross streets, remember that numbers increase east or west from 5th Ave., which runs north–south.

Ave. A... *add 3*
Ave. B...*add 3*
Ave. C...*add 3*
Ave. D...*add 3*
1st Ave....*add 3*
2nd Ave....*add 3*
3rd Ave.... *add 10*
4th Ave.... *add 8*
5th Ave.
Up to 200...*add 13*
Up to 400...*add 16*
Up to 600...*add 18*
Up to 775...*add 20*
From 775 to 1286... *cancel last figure and subt. 18*
Ave. of the Americas...*subt. 12*
7th Ave....*add 12*
Above 110th St... *add 20*
8th Ave....*add 9*
9th Ave....*add 13*
10th Ave....*add 14*
Amsterdam Ave....*add 59*
Audubon Ave....*add 165*
Broadway (23–192 Sts.)...*subt. 30*
Columbus Ave....*add 60*
Convent Ave....*add 127*
Central Park West... *divide house number by 10 and add 60*
Edgecombe Ave....*add 134*
Ft. Washington Ave....*add 158*
Lenox Ave.....*add 110*
Lexington Ave....*add 22*
Madison Ave....*add 27*
Manhattan Ave....*add 100*
Park Ave....*add 34*
Park Ave. South...*add 8*
Pleasant Ave....*add 101*
Riverside Drive... *divide house number by 10 and add 72 up to 165 Street*
St. Nicholas Ave....*add 110*
Wadsworth Ave....*add 173*
West End Ave....*add 59*
York Ave....*add 4*

the proximate and roughly parallel Greenwich Street and Greenwich Avenue, the transformation of Leroy Street into St. Luke's Place for one block before reverting to Leroy, and the general confusion engendered by East Broadway, West Broadway, and just plain Broadway.

Logic won't help you below 14th Street; only a good street map and good directions will.

You may also be confused by the way New Yorkers use "uptown" and "downtown." These terms refer both to locations and to directions. Uptown means north of wherever you are at the moment; downtown means south. Yet uptown and downtown are also geographical areas of the city. Unfortunately, there is no consensus about where these areas are: "Downtown" may mean anyplace from the tip of Lower Manhattan through Chelsea; it depends on the orientation of the speaker.

A similar situation exists with "East Side" and "West Side." Someone may characterize a location as being "on the East Side," meaning somewhere east of Fifth Avenue. A hotel described as being "on the West Side" may be located on West 42nd Street. But when many New Yorkers speak of the East Side or the West Side, they have in mind the respective areas above 59th Street (the southern boundary of Central Park), on either side of the park. Admittedly, the usage is not precise; you should be prepared for misunderstandings.

Tour 1: Midtown: Rockefeller Center

Numbers in the margin correspond with points of interest on the Midtown Manhattan map.

1 The heart of midtown Manhattan is **Rockefeller Center,** a complex of 19 buildings occupying nearly 22 acres of prime real estate between Fifth and Seventh avenues and 47th and 52nd streets. Built during the Great Depression of the 1930s by John D. Rockefeller, Jr., this city-within-a-city is the capital of the communications industry, with the headquarters for a TV network (NBC), major publishing companies (Time-Warner, McGraw-Hill, and Simon & Schuster), and the world's largest news-gather-

Midtown Manhattan

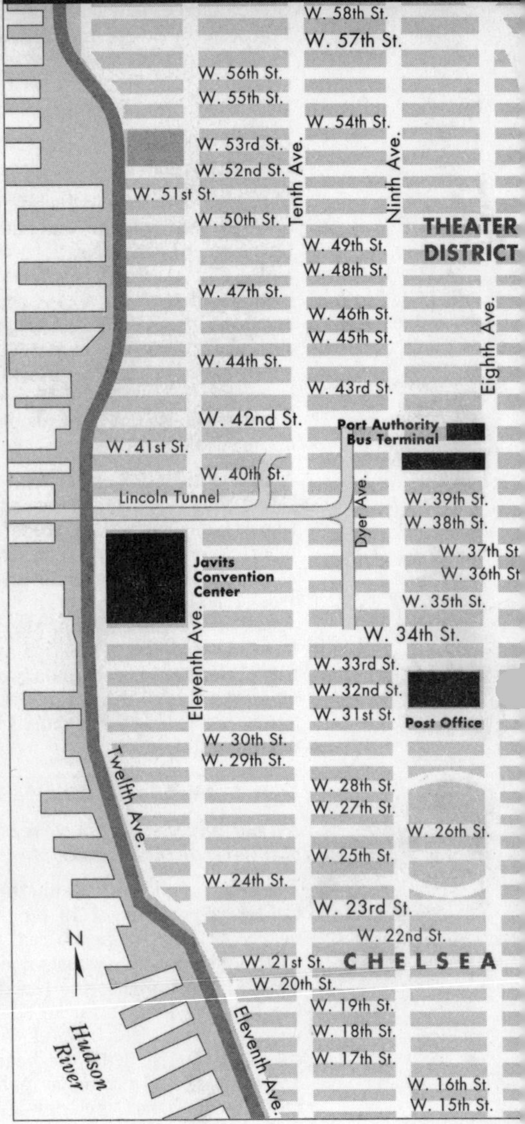

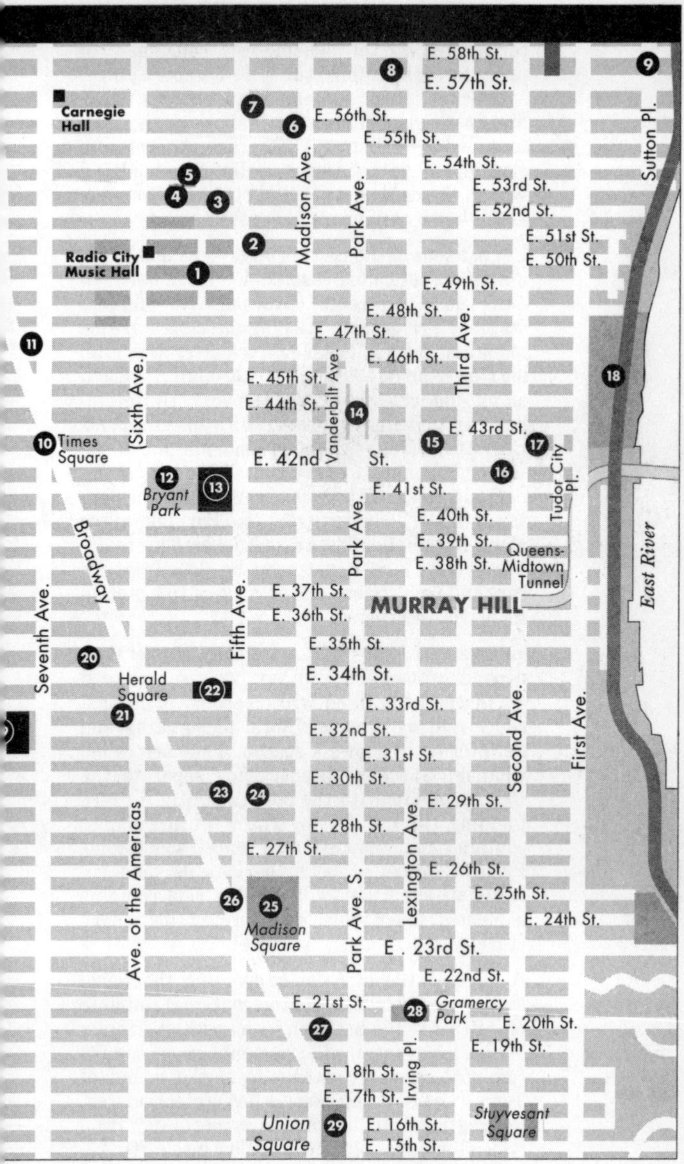
E. 58th St.
E. 57th St.
Carnegie Hall
E. 56th St.
E. 55th St.
E. 54th St.
E. 53rd St.
E. 52nd St.
E. 51st St.
E. 50th St.
E. 49th St.
E. 48th St.
E. 47th St.
E. 46th St.
E. 45th St.
E. 44th St.
E. 43rd St.
E. 42nd St.
E. 41st St.
E. 40th St.
E. 39th St.
E. 38th St.
E. 37th St.
E. 36th St.
E. 35th St.
E. 34th St.
E. 33rd St.
E. 32nd St.
E. 31st St.
E. 30th St.
E. 29th St.
E. 28th St.
E. 27th St.
E. 26th St.
E. 25th St.
E. 24th St.
E . 23rd St.
E. 22nd St.
E. 21st St.
E. 20th St.
E. 19th St.
E. 18th St.
E. 17th St.
E. 16th St.
E. 15th St.
Sutton Pl.
Madison Ave.
Park Ave.
Radio City Music Hall
Third Ave.
Vanderbilt Ave.
(Sixth Ave.)
Times Square
Bryant Park
Tudor City Pl.
Queens-Midtown Tunnel
East River
Broadway
Seventh Ave.
Fifth Ave.
MURRAY HILL
Herald Square
Second Ave.
First Ave.
Ave. of the Americas
Lexington Ave.
Park Ave. S.
Madison Square
Gramercy Park
Irving Pl.
Union Square
Stuyvesant Square
1
2
3
4
5
6
7
8
9
10
11
12
13
14
15
16
17
18
20
21
22
23
24
25
26
27
28
29

ing ganization, the Associated Press. It is an international center housing the consulates of many foreign nations, the U.S. passport office, and ticket offices for numerous airlines. Most human needs—restaurants, shoe repair, doctors, barbers, banks, post office, bookstores, clothing, variety stores—can be accommodated within the center, and all parts of the complex are linked by underground passageways.

Begin a tour at the ice rink on **Lower Plaza** along a little street called Rockefeller Plaza between 49th and 50th streets. Crowned by a gold-leaf statue of Prometheus stealing the sacred fire for mankind, this famous New York attraction is an ice rink from late September through April and an outdoor cafe the rest of the year. In December the plaza is decorated with an enormous Christmas tree. On the Esplanade above the Lower Plaza, flags of the United Nations' members alternate with flags of the states. Incidentally, those "Private Street, No Parking" signs along Rockefeller Plaza aren't jokes: This really is a private street that must be closed to both cars and pedestrians one day a year to maintain its private status.

Just east of Lower Plaza are the **Channel Gardens,** a promenade with six pools surrounded by flower beds filled with seasonal plantings, conceived by artists, floral designers, and sculptors—10 shows a season. They are called Channel Gardens because they separate the British building (to the north) and the French building (to the south). The French building contains the **Librairie de France,** which sells French-language books, periodicals, and records; its surprisingly large basement contains a Spanish bookstore and foreign dictionary store.

A huge statue of Atlas supporting the world stands sentry before the **International Building** on Fifth Avenue between 50th and 51st streets. With a lobby inspired by ancient Greece and fitted with Grecian marble from the island of Tenos, the building houses foreign consulates, international airlines, and a passport office from which lines of applicants overflow into Fifth Avenue throughout the summer.

2 Across Fifth Avenue stands the Gothic-style **St. Patrick's,** the Roman Catholic cathedral of New York. Dedicated to the patron saint of the Irish—then and now one of New York's principal ethnic groups—the white marble and stone structure was begun in 1858, consecrated in 1879, and completed in 1906. Among the statues in the alcoves around the nave is a striking modern rendering of the American saint, Mother Seton.

One of Rockefeller Center's main attractions is the **GE Building** (formerly the RCA Building, until GE acquired RCA in 1986), the 70-story tower that occupies the block bounded by Rockefeller Plaza, Avenue of the Americas (which New Yorkers call Sixth Avenue), and 49th and 50th streets. The building is headquarters for NBC. One way to see what goes on up there is to request free tickets to live-audience shows taped in Manhattan at NBC—currently *Late Night with David Letterman, Saturday Night Live,* and *Donahue*—by writing NBC Tickets, 30 Rockefeller Plaza, New York, NY 10112. (Unfortunately, "Letterman" is usually booked solid for a year and a half in advance, *Donahue* for about six months, but both shows have standby waiting lists; "Saturday Night" uses a lottery system.) Or you might take a tour of the NBC studios: One leaves every 15 minutes, 9:30–4, Monday through Saturday, and Sundays during the summer; Thursdays 9:30–8 (cost: $7.25). And you can buy a T-shirt, ashtray, frisbee, or other paraphernalia bearing logos from your favorite programs at a boutique in the magnificent black granite lobby. Look up at the ceiling mural above the Rockefeller Plaza entrance: The figure seems to be facing you no matter where you stand.

NBC isn't the only network headquartered in Manhattan. CBS is located in a black monolith, popularly called Black Rock, at Sixth Avenue and 53rd Street. ABC, once a close neighbor, has now moved its main office to 66th Street on the West Side.

Escalators in the GE Building will take you to the marble catacombs that connect the various components of Rockefeller Center. A lot goes on down under: There are restaurants in all price ranges, from the chic American Festival Café, alongside the skating rink, to McDonald's; an historical exhibit; a post office and clean public washrooms (both scarce in Midtown); and just about every kind of store. To find your way around, consult the strategically placed directories or obtain the free "Shops and Services Guide" at the GE building information desk (where you can also pick up a brochure for a self-guided walking tour). *Center*, a free bimonthly magazine containing articles about Rockefeller Center, a calendar of events, and capsule descriptions of the restaurants, is available in the lobbies of most of the buildings.

Across 50th Street from the GE Building is America's largest indoor theater, the 6,000-seat **Radio City Music Hall.** Home of the fabulous Rockettes chorus line (which actually started out in St. Louis in 1925), Radio City was built as a movie theater with live shows; today it produces concerts, Christmas and Easter extravaganzas, awards presentations, and other special events. On most days you can tour the premises (tel. 212/632–4041 for prices and availability).

Components of the Rockefeller Center community along Sixth Avenue include the 51-story **McGraw-Hill Building,** between 48th and 49th streets. Its lower plaza contains a 50-foot steel sun triangle that points to the seasonal positions of the sun at noon, and a pool that demonstrates the relative size of the planets.

Time Out For supercasual eating when the weather is good, the **Sixth Avenue food vendors** near Rockefeller Center offer the best selection in the city. Most à la "cart" diners eschew the hot dog as being too pedestrian when they can just as easily have tacos, falafel, souvlaki, tempura, Indian curry, Afghani kofta kebabs, or Caribbean beef jerky. Locations change periodically, so look around until you find what you like. Food carts are licensed and inspected by the Department of Health. And the price is right; no dish is more than $5, and most cost much less. For seating, perch on the benches and low walls in the plazas beside the massive Sixth Avenue office towers.

---

3 On the same side of Fifth Avenue, the **Museum of Television and Radio** presents special screenings, usually retrospectives of the work of a particular radio or TV star or of an era in broadcasting history. The museum also offers its stupendous collection of more than 25,000 TV shows, 10,000 commercials, and 15,000 radio programs for individual screening. *25 W. 52nd St., tel. 212/752–7684. Suggested contribution: $4 adults, $3 students, $2 senior citizens and children under 13. Open Tues. noon–8; Wed.–Sat. noon–5.*

Between Sixth and Fifth avenues on 53rd Street
4 is a mini Museum Row. The **American Craft Museum** spotlights the work of contemporary American and overseas craftspersons working in clay, glass, fiber, wood, metal, paper. *40 W. 53rd St., tel. 212/956–3535. Admission: $3.50 adults, $1.50 students and senior citizens. Open Tues. 10–8; Wed.–Sun. 10–5.*

5 The **Museum of Modern Art** (MOMA) is a bright and airy four-story structure built around a secluded sculpture garden. All the important movements of modern art are represented here. After only a quick look-see, you'll be able to drop terms like Cubism, Surrealism, Abstract Expressionism, Minimalism, and Postmodernism as though you've known them all your life. Some of the world's most famous paintings are hung on the second floor: Van Gogh's *Starry Night*, Picasso's *Les Demoiselles d'Avignon*, Matisse's *Dance*. The superstars of American art appear on the third floor: Andrew Wyeth, Andy Warhol, Jackson Pollock, Frank Stella, Mark Rothko—to name a few. Don't miss the classic office furniture and Paris subway bench in the fourth-floor Architecture and Design Collection. Afternoon and evening film showings, mostly foreign films and classics, are free with the price of admission; tickets are distributed in the lobby, and on some days they go fast. Programs change daily; call 212/708–9500 for a schedule. *11 W. 53rd St., tel. 212/708–9400. Admission: $7 adults, $4 students, $4 senior citizens; children under 16 free. Pay what you wish Thurs. 5–9. Open daily 11–6; Thurs. 11–9; closed Wed.*

Tour 2: Midtown: Fifth Avenue

The stretch of Fifth Avenue between Rockefeller Center and 57th Street glitters with world-famous shops. The list begins with **Saks Fifth Avenue** (Fifth Ave. at 50th St.), the flagship of the national chain. Another big-name store is **Gucci**—actually two Guccis, on adjacent corners of Fifth Avenue and 54th Street. **Bijan** (699 Fifth Ave.) sells wildly expensive men's Continental clothing—by appointment only. Health warnings and no-smoking ordinances notwithstanding, **Nat Sherman** (711 Fifth Ave.) continues to market his own brands of cigarettes, cigars, and smoking accessories from his clubby shop.

Steuben Glass occupies a ground-floor showroom of a green-glass tower at Fifth Avenue and 56th Street. Across the street, **Harry Winston** (718 Fifth Ave.) has a spectacular selection of fine jewelry. Next door is the recently relocated designer fashion store **Henri Bendel** (712 5th Ave.) with its René Lalique art-glass windows. **Tiffany & Co.** (727 Fifth Ave., at 57th St.) is less intimidating and perhaps somewhat less expensive than you may fear.

Take a serenity break in **St. Thomas's Church** (Fifth Ave. at 53rd St.), an Episcopal institution that has occupied the site since 1911. The impressive huge stone reredos behind the altar holds the statues of more than 50 apostles, saints, martyrs, missionaries, and church figures.

A block east, on Madison Avenue and 55th Street, you can pop into the post-deregulation
6 home of Ma Bell in the new **AT&T World Headquarters,** designed by architect Philip Johnson. Unlike the sterile ice-cube-tray buildings of Sixth Avenue, AT&T's rose granite columns, its regilded statue of the winged *Golden Boy* in the lobby, and its peculiar "Chippendale" roof have earned it its sobriquet as the first Post-Modern skyscraper. An adjacent structure houses the **AT&T InfoQuest Center,** a Post-Modern museum of communications technology. Entrants receive an access card on which they encode their names and then use to operate displays on light-

wave communication, microelectronics, and computer software. Displays are neither terribly technical nor (on behalf of AT&T) zealously self-serving. Some exhibits, such as those where you program your own music video and rearrange a scrambled picture of your face, are downright entertaining. *Madison Ave. at 56th St., tel. 212/605–5555. Admission free. Open Wed.–Sun. 10–6; Tues. 10–9.*

Cross 56th Street to the **IBM Building,** with its fragrant and inviting public atrium (*see* Off the Beaten Track, below). A passage connects it to its next-door neighbor, but you'll do better to
7 walk around the corner and encounter **Trump Tower** through the grand Fifth Avenue entrance. Trump Tower is an exclusive 68-story, dark-glass apartment and office building. What's open to the public is a six-story shopping atrium paneled in pinkishorange marble and trimmed with high-gloss brass. A fountain cascades against one wall, drowning out the clamor of the city. In further contrast to the real world, every inch of Trump Tower is kept gleamingly shined, and security is omnipresent but discreet. Shops are chic and tony, among them Cartier, Bucellati, Abercrombie & Fitch, and Asprey, and the public rest rooms in the basement are invitingly clean and spacious.

Time Out The intimate front bar at **Jean Lafitte** (68 W. 58th St., tel. 212/751–2323) is an unusually relaxed place for this busy area of New York.

Tour 3: Midtown: 57th Street

Don't consider hunting for bargains in the exclusive shops and galleries of 57th Street. A recent survey determined that merchants here paid the world's highest ground-floor retail rents: $425 per square foot, edging out Tokyo's Ginza ($400) and Fifth Avenue between 52nd and 58th streets ($375). In general, the high costs are passed along to the consumer.

Occupying the span of Fifth Avenue between 57th Street and the Plaza Hotel, is **Bergdorf Goodman** with its women's designer boutiques and, across the avenue, a complete men's store.

Van Cleef & Arpels jewelers is located within Bergdorf's 57th Street corner.

Buy the classic trenchcoat with the distinctive plaid lining straight from the source, at no savings whatsoever, at **Burberrys Ltd.** (9 E. 57th St.). **Hermès** (11 E. 57th St.) is a small, dignified, and intermittently chic Paris leather shop. Occupying the former site of Bonwit Teller, **Galeries Lafayette New York** (4–10 E. 57th St.), a New World version of the Paris original, is a recent addition to the 57th Street shopping scene.

Louis Vuitton (51 E. 57th St.) stamps its familiar "LV" monogram on its luggage, which it produced first for the ocean-liner crowd and later for the jet set. **The Gazebo** (127 E. 57th St.) sells country-style home furnishings such as quilts, wicker work, and rag rugs. Best known now for the catalog through which it distributes gizmos for people who can afford anything, **Hammacher Schlemmer** (147 E. 57th St.), founded in 1848, has stood at this spot since 1926.

In two sleekly Art Deco subterranean levels,
8 the recently opened **Place des Antiquaires** (125 E. 57th St.) is an ultra-high-class shopping mall with several dozen of the city's top art and antiques dealers. You may find the prices out of your league but it costs nothing to look.

When you've had your fill of shopping, walk to
9 58th Street and head east across **Sutton Place** until you can go no farther. There you will find the romantic spot overlooking the East River and the Queensboro (or 59th Street) Bridge where Woody Allen and Diane Keaton talked the night away in *Manhattan*. Cinema trivia buffs please note that no bench presently occupies the precise spot where Woody and Diane sat; however, several benches in Sutton Place Park afford a comparable view.

Tour 4: Midtown: 42nd Street

Crossroads of the World, Great White Way, the
10 New Year's Eve Capital of America, **Times Square** remains one of New York's principal energy centers. Like most New York City "squares," Times Square is a triangle, this one

formed by Broadway, Seventh Avenue, and 42nd Street. The square itself is occupied by the former Times Tower, now simply **One Times Square Plaza.** On its roof, workmen still lower the 200-pound New Year's Eve ball down the flagpole by hand, just as they have since 1908.

At Duffy Square, on 47th Street between
11 Broadway and Seventh Avenue, the **TKTS booth** of the Theater Development Fund sells half-price (plus $2 per ticket service charge) day-of-performance tickets to Broadway and Off-Broadway shows. Signboards on the front of the booth list the shows available that day, and the offerings fluctuate greatly. Some nights (or matinees) it seems that almost every show in town is up for grabs; at other times there may be nothing but a few long-running hits and some sleepers. The lines may look long, but they move surprisingly fast. TKTS accepts only cash or traveler's checks. *Tel. 212/354–5800. Open 10–2 for Wed. and Sat. matinees; 3–8 for evening performances; noon–8 for Sun. matinee and evening shows. TKTS booths are open earlier in the day at 2 World Trade Center and in front of Borough Hall in Brooklyn.*

Most Broadway theaters are located on the streets west of Broadway from 52nd Street to 44th Street. The offices of ***The New York Times*** (229 W. 43rd St.), the institution that gave the area its name, occupy much of the block between Seventh and Eighth avenues.

42nd Street is the title of a long-running musical (and an earlier movie) that evokes the glamour and excitement of the New York stage. Today a group of thriving Off-Broadway playhouses, often called **Theater Row,** between Ninth and Tenth avenues are the only live theater on 42nd Street; the block between Seventh and Eighth avenues that was once the heart of the theater district is now a disreputable strip of porno shops, movie houses, and loiterers, all marking time while the city assembles the pieces of a redevelopment project that will transform the area. The most prominent vestige of the now legendary 42nd Street is the **New Amsterdam** (214 W. 42nd St.), a designated landmark that opened in 1903. Today the New Amsterdam is "dark," but in its prime the opulent facility, with a second, rooftop theater, showcased the likes of Eddie Cantor, Will Rogers, Fanny Brice, and the Ziegfeld Girls.

Heading east on 42nd Street, you'll pass **Hotaling's News** (142 W. 42nd St., tel. 212/840-1868), where the front compartment of the bustling little shop carries more than 220 daily newspapers from throughout the USA, the publications generally only a day or two old. The rear section stocks current newspapers, magazines, and foreign language books from more than 40 countries.

Bryant Park and the New York Public Library occupy the entire block bounded by 42nd Street, Fifth Avenue, 40th Street, and Sixth Avenue. Named for the poet and editor William Cullen Bryant (1794–1878), Bryant Park was the site of America's first World's Fair, the Crystal Palace Exhibition of 1853–1854. For a while the park was getting rather shaggy, but an elaborate landscape and restoration program should be completed by the time you read this.

12 Inside the park, along 42nd Street, **Bryant Park Half-Price Tickets** sells same-day tickets for music and dance performances. Like theater TKTS, they go for half-price, plus $2 per ticket service charge, cash or traveler's checks only. *Open Tues., Thurs., Fri. noon–2 and 3–7; Wed. and Sat. 11–2 and 3–7; Sun. noon–6; tel. 212/382–2323 for daily listings.*

Time Out A cafeteria on the 18th floor of the **City University Graduate Center** provides a serene setting for a reasonably priced repast, from a snack or salad-bar salad to a full meal. *33 W. 42nd St., tel. 212/642–2013. Open weekdays 10–8.*

A ground-level passage through the building, connecting 42nd and 43rd streets, often contains art exhibits: Walk through it and behold the offices of *The New Yorker* magazine at 25 W. 43rd Street.

---

13 The **New York Public Library** is one of the largest research libraries in the world. Ascend the sweeping staircase between the two crouching Tennessee marble lions—dubbed "Patience"

and "Fortitude" by Mayor Fiorello La Guardia, who visited the facility to "read between the lions"—and you enter a distinguished achievement of Beaux Arts design (note the triple bronze front doors), an art gallery, and a museum. The research hub of the 85-branch New York Public Library system, the main building displays a Gilbert Stuart portrait of George Washington, Charles Dickens's desk, and Jefferson's own handwritten copy of the Declaration of Independence. Periodic exhibitions mounted at the library focus on literary matters. Free one-hour tours, each as different as the library volunteer who leads it, are given Monday through Saturday at 11 AM and 2 PM. *Tel. 212/930–0800. Open Mon.–Wed. 10–8:45, Thurs.–Sat. 10–5:45.*

14 Continue east on 42nd Street to **Grand Central Terminal** (never "station," since all runs begin or end here). Constructed between 1903 and 1913, this Manhattan landmark was originally designed by a Minnesota architectural firm and later gussied up with Beaux Arts ornamentation. Make sure you notice the three huge windows separated by columns, and the Beaux Arts clock and sculpture on the facade above 42nd Street. The 12-story ceiling of the cavernous Main Concourse displays the constellations of the Zodiac. *Tel. 212/935–3960. Free tours Wed. at 12:30 PM.*

Two facilities of note stand at adjacent corners of Park Avenue and 42nd Street, directly opposite Grand Central. On the southwest corner, the **Whitney Museum of American Art at Philip Morris** (120 Park Ave.) occupies the ground floor of the Philip Morris Building. Each year this free branch of the Whitney (*see* Tour 7, below) presents five successive exhibitions of 20th-century painting and sculpture. An espresso bar and seating areas make it a much more agreeable place to rest and reconnoiter than anywhere in Grand Central.

The second floor of the building on the southeast corner of 42nd Street and Park Avenue houses ticket counters for most major U.S. airlines. Buses to three New York airports depart from just outside the Park Avenue entrance. Next door is the main office of the **Bowery Savings Bank** (110 E. 42nd St.), whose massive arches and 70-foot-high marble columns give it the grand presence of a medieval castle.

Ask New Yorkers to name their favorite skyscraper, and the response you'll hear most often
15 will be the **Chrysler Building** at 42nd Street and Lexington Avenue. The Chrysler Corporation itself is long gone, yet the graceful shaft that culminates in a stainless steel point still captivates the eye and the imagination. The building has no observation deck, but you can examine the elegant dark lobby faced with African marble and covered with a ceiling mural that honors transportation and human endeavor.

New York's blue-collar tabloid is produced in the
16 **Daily News Building** (220 E. 42nd St.), an Art Deco tower designed with brown-brick spandrels and windows to make it seem loftier than its 37 stories. The lobby features a revolving illuminated globe, 12 feet in diameter. The floor is a gigantic compass on which bronze lines indicate air mileage from principal world cities to New York. A small gallery displays *News* photos.

17 The **Ford Foundation Building** (320 E. 43rd St.) encloses a 12-story, one-third acre greenhouse. With a terraced garden, a still pool, and a couple dozen full-grown trees as centerpieces, the Ford garden is open to the public—for tranquillity, not for picnics—weekdays from 9 to 5.

Climb the steps along 42nd Street between First and Second avenues to enter **Tudor City,** a self-contained complex of a dozen buildings in the Tudor Gothic style, featuring half-timbering and lots of stained glass. Constructed between 1925 and 1928, the apartments of this residential enclave originally had no east-side windows, lest the tenants be forced to gaze at the slaughterhouses, breweries, and glue factories then located along the East River.

Walk north across the overpass above 42nd Street and turn east on 43rd Street until the street ends in a terrace overlooking the United Nations Headquarters. The terrace stands at the head of the Sharansky Steps (for Natan, formerly Anatoly, the Soviet dissident), which run along the Isaiah Wall (inscribed, "They Shall Beat Their Swords Into Plowshares"), and overlooks Ralph J. Bunche Park (for the black American former UN undersecretary) and Raoul Wallenberg Walk (for the Swedish diplomat and World War II hero).

18 The **United Nations Headquarters** complex occupies a lushly landscaped riverside tract along First Avenue between 42nd and 48th streets. A line of flagpoles with banners representing the current roster of 159 member nations stands before the striking 550-foot slab of the Secretariat Building. The interior corridors overflow with imaginatively diverse artwork donated by member nations. Free tickets to most sessions are available on a first-come, first-served basis 15 minutes before sessions begin; pick them up in the General Assembly lobby. Visitors can take early luncheon in the Delegates Dining Room or eat anytime in a public coffee shop. *Tel. 212/963–7713. One-hour tours leave the General Assembly lobby every 15–20 minutes, daily 9:15–4:45. Admission: $5.50 adults, $3.50 students. Children under 5 not permitted.*

Tour 5: Midtown: South of 42nd Street

The gateway to the city for Amtrak passengers and commuters from New Jersey and Long Is-
19 land, **Penn Station** is a convenient place to begin a tour of lower Midtown. However, it is not in itself a particularly felicitous spot. Unattractive, unsavory, and underground, it serves as an embarrassing reminder of the grand old Penn Station that fell to the wrecking ball in 1963. (If you arrive in New York at Penn Station, do not under any circumstances surrender your baggage to the characters hovering about its many exits: They are not porters; their business is extortion and theft.)

19 **Madison Square Garden** (tel. 212/465–6741), here in its fourth incarnation, is located directly above Penn Station. Home of the New York Knickerbockers (pro basketball) and the New York Rangers (pro hockey), the Garden lights up almost every night with dog and cat shows, college basketball, wrestling, rock concerts, cir-

cuses, and other events and expositions; boxing takes place in the smaller Felt Forum. One of the last remaining bowling alleys in Manhattan, the 48-lane Madison Square Garden Bowling Center, is located just above the ticket office.

Head north from Penn Station on Seventh Avenue, and you enter New York's tumultuous **Garment District:** Street signs declare the stretch of Seventh Avenue between 31st and 41st streets "Fashion Avenue." The Garment District teems with warehouses, workshops, and showrooms that manufacture and finish mostly women's and children's clothing. On weekdays the streets are crowded with trucks and the sidewalks swarm with daredevil deliverymen hauling garment racks between factories and subcontractors.

20 Perhaps to inspire the garment dealers, **Macy's,** the world's largest department store under one roof, occupies the entire block bounded by Broadway, Seventh Avenue, and 34th and 35th streets. Made world-famous by *Miracle on 34th Street* and as the destination of the Thanksgiving Day parade, Macy's is still good for a few surprises: At the gourmet food shop in The Cellar, someone is usually distributing free samples of something good to eat (lower level). Other popular spots are the New York, New York souvenir boutique (first floor); the Metropolitan Museum gift shop (mezzanine); and Center Stage Recording Studio, where you can record yourself singing over the instrumental tracks of your favorite hits (fourth floor).

With the demise of the New York Gimbel's, one of the few other major retail enterprises on Herald Square is **Herald Center** (Sixth Ave. at 34th St.), a glittering shopping mall. Each level of the streamlined center bears the name of a New York neighborhood (SoHo, Greenwich Village, etc.); most stores are high-toned branches of national chains (Ann Taylor, Ylang-Ylang, Caswell-Massey).

A block south of Macy's you'll find the nine-story
21 **A&S Plaza** (Sixth Ave. at 33rd St.) in the old Gimbel's location. The 120 shops and restaurants found here are anchored by the Abraham & Straus department store.

22 The **Empire State Building** may no longer be the world's tallest, but it is certainly the world's best-loved skyscraper. The Art Deco playground for King Kong opened in 1931 after only about a year of construction. More than 16,000 people work in the building, and more than 2.5 million people a year visit the 86th-floor and 102nd-floor observatories. At night the top 30 stories are illuminated with colors appropriate to the season (red and green around Christmas; orange and brown for Halloween). *Fifth Ave. at 34th St., tel. 212/736–3100. Admission: $3.50 adults, $1.75 children under 12. Open daily 9:30 AM–midnight.*

Continue south on Fifth Avenue to 29th Street
23 and the **Marble Collegiate Church** (1854), a marble-fronted structure built for the Reformed Protestant Dutch Congregation first organized in 1628 by Peter Minuit, the canny Dutchman who bought Manhattan from the Indians for $24. In modern times its pulpit was occupied by Dr. Norman Vincent Peale (*The Power of Positive Thinking)*, its pastor from 1932 to 1984.

24 Go east on 29th Street to the **Church of the Transfiguration** (1 E. 29th St.), which is much better known as the Little Church Around the Corner. Set back in a shrub-filled New York version of an old English churchyard, it won its memorable appellation in 1870 when other area churches refused to bury an actor and colleague of the well-known thespian Joseph Jefferson. Jefferson was directed to the "little church around the corner," which did that sort of thing, and the Episcopal institution has welcomed literary and show-biz types ever since.

Bordered by Fifth Avenue, Broadway, Madison
25 Avenue, 23rd and 26th streets, **Madison Square** was the site (circa 1845) of New York's first baseball games. Though recently rehabilitated with modern sculpture, new benches, and a playground, the most interesting aspects of Madison Square are found along its perimeter.

The block at 26th Street and Madison Avenue, now occupied by the ornate **New York Life Insurance Building,** was the site of the second (1890–1925) Madison Square Garden. The old Garden was designed by the architect and playboy Stanford White, who was shot on the Garden roof by Harry K. Thaw, the jealous husband of the actress Evelyn Nesbit. This lurid episode was more or less accurately depicted in the movie *Ragtime*, scenes of which were filmed on the then-cobblestoned street in front of the **Appellate Division of the State Supreme Court** (Madison Ave. at 25th St.). The roof balustrade of this imposing, white-marble Corinthian structure depicts great lawmakers of the past: Moses, Justinian, Confucius, and others. **The Metropolitan Life Insurance Tower** (Madison Ave. between 23rd and 24th Sts.) re-creates the campanile of St. Mark's in Venice.

26 The Renaissance-style **Flatiron Building,** by architect Daniel Burnham, occupies the triangular lot formed by Broadway, Fifth Avenue, and 23rd Street. Soon after the three-sided 20-story skyscraper was built in 1902, it became a symbol of New York on the rise. Now it lends its name to the Flatiron District that lies to the south, an area of photographers' studios, residential lofts, and advertising agencies.

Continue down Broadway and turn east on 20th
27 Street to the **Theodore Roosevelt Birthplace,** a reconstructed Victorian brownstone where Teddy lived until he was 15 years old. Before becoming President, Roosevelt was New York City police commissioner and the governor of New York State. The house contains Victorian period rooms and Roosevelt memorabilia; a selection of videos about the namesake of the teddy bear are shown on request. *28 E. 20th St., tel. 212/260–1616. Admission: $1. Open Wed.–Sun. 9–5; last tour 3:30.*

Next door to Roosevelt's home is an interesting shop called **Darts Unlimited, Limited** (30 E. 20th St.), which sells nothing but professional English darts, dartboards, patches, and other dart accessories.

Time Out **Miss Kim's** typifies a kind of dining establishment unique to Manhattan. At this combination grocery store, salad bar, and cafeteria, you obtain your food from a huge 50-item salad table, sandwich bar, steam table with hot foods, pastry counter, or directly from the shelves. Countermen serve hot drinks (including espresso); you take cold drinks (including beer) straight from the cooler. After you weigh and pay, you can either take your meal out or climb to seats on a mezzanine. Similar places exist all over town. *270 Park Ave. S. Open 24 hrs.*

Just east of Park Avenue South, between 20th
28 and 21st streets, lies **Gramercy Park,** a picture-perfect city park complete with flower beds, bird feeders, sundials, cozy benches, and a statue of the actor Edwin Booth portraying Hamlet. It stays nice because it's surrounded by a locked cast-iron fence and only residents of the property around the park possess keys. Laid out in 1831 according to a design inspired by London's residential squares, Gramercy Park is surrounded by interesting structures.

Begin at the northeast corner and head clockwise. The white terra-cotta apartment building at 36 Gramercy Park East is guarded by concrete knights in silver-paint armor. The turreted red-brick building at 34 Gramercy Park East was one of the city's first cooperative apartment houses. The austere gray-brown Friends Meeting House at 28 Gramercy Park South became The Brotherhood Synagogue in 1974.

Mrs. Stuyvesant Fish, a society doyenne remembered as the fearless iconoclast who reduced the time of formal dinner parties from several hours to 50 minutes, resided at No. 19. Edwin Booth lived at No. 16, which he remodeled in the early 1880s to serve as an actor's club, The Players Club. The site of the **National Arts Club** (15 Gramercy Park South) was the home of Samuel Tilden, a governor of New York and the Democratic presidential candidate who in 1876 received more votes than Rutherford B. Hayes, who won the presidency.

Return to Park Avenue South and continue
29 south to **Union Square,** the area between Park and Broadway, 14th and 17th streets. During the early part of the century, Union Square was a popular patch of green and the site of political demonstrations. Over the years it deteriorated into a habitat of drug dealers and kindred unde-

sirables; until a massive renewal program in the 1980s transformed it into one of the city's most attractive miniparks.

If possible, visit Union Square on greenmarket days (Wednesday, Friday, Saturday), when farmers from all over the Northeast bring their goods to the big town. Farmers, including some Pennsylvania Dutch and latter-day hippies, sell their own produce, homemade baked goods, cheeses, cider, New York State wines, even fish and meat. If the prices aren't much lower than those in stores, the quality and freshness are much greater. When the weather allows, the benches of Union Square make a great site for a city-style picnic.

Tour 6: Upper West Side

Numbers in the margin correspond with points of interest on the Upper West Side map.

Diversity may be the quality that best characterizes the Upper West Side. A once-fashionable district that had become a multiethnic neighborhood of families and intellectuals, the Upper West Side now attracts young professionals who can afford to live anywhere. Lincoln Center is the cultural anchor, Columbus Avenue the newly fashionable boutique and restaurant strip. Many of the old residents decry the changes that have befallen the neighborhood, but then contentiousness is another characteristic of the Upper West Side.

1 The West Side story begins at **Columbus Circle,** where a statue of Christopher himself crowns a stately pillar at the intersection of Broadway, Eighth Avenue, Central Park West, and Central Park South. Columbus Circle is a good place to begin any tour of New York, for it is the location of the **New York Convention and Visitors Bureau.** Count on the bureau for brochures; bus and subway maps; hotel, restaurant, and shopping guides; a seasonal calendar of events; free TV-show tickets (sometimes) and discounts for Broadway shows; and sound advice. The New York City Department of Cultural Affairs operates an art gallery on the second floor. *2 Columbus Circle, tel. 212/397–8222. Open weekdays 9–6, weekends 10–6.*

American Museum of Natural History, **4**
Cathedral of St. John the Divine, **10**
Columbia University, **11**
Columbus Circle, **1**
The Dakota, **2**
Grant's Tomb, **13**
Hayden Planetarium, **4**
Lincoln Center, **5**
Museum of American Folk Art, **6**
New York Historical Society, **3**
Riverside Church, **12**
Soldiers and Sailors Monument, **8**
Symphony Space, **9**
Verdi Square, **7**

Upper West Side

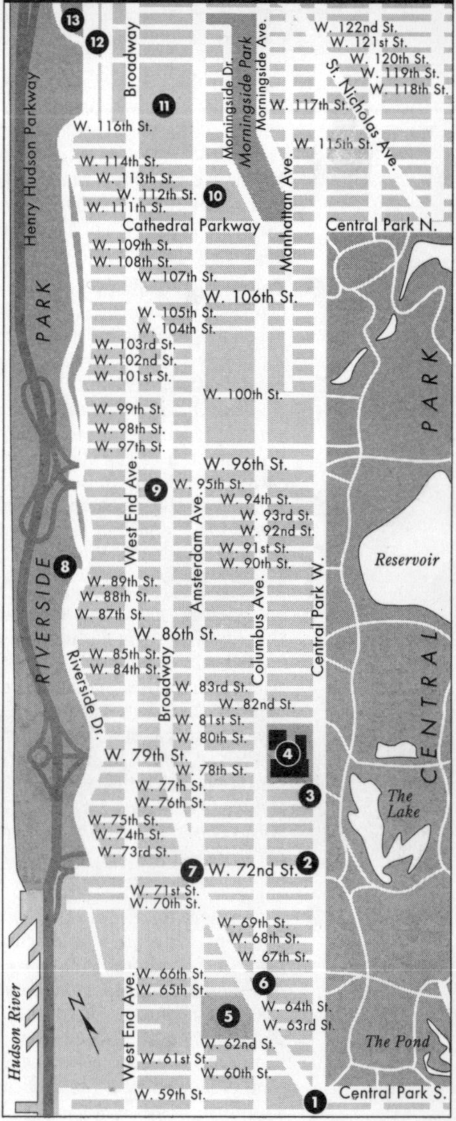

Central Park West

Walk north from Columbus Circle along Central Park West and you quickly reach the haunted apartment house of the film *Ghostbusters* (55 Central Park West at 66th St.). Just inside the park, at 66th Street, is **Tavern on the Green,** a landmark spot for romantic indoor and outdoor dining. The stretch of Central Park roadway between the restaurant and the verdant Sheep Meadow is the finish line for the New York Marathon (the first Sunday in November). It's also the start and finish of a five-mile "fun run" that begins on the stroke of the New Year.

2 The stately **Dakota** presides at the corner of Central Park West and 72nd Street. One of the first fashionable West Side apartment buildings, this powerful, relatively squat structure is now better known as the place where *Rosemary's Baby* was filmed and John Lennon was shot. Directly across Central Park West, a hilly stretch of parkland has been designated **Strawberry Fields** in Lennon's memory. A black-and-white-tile mosaic containing the word "Imagine," another Lennon song title, is embedded in one of the paths.

3 The city's oldest museum, the **New-York Historical Society,** preserves what was unique about the city's past, including the quaint hyphen in New-York. Along with changing exhibits of American history and art, the museum displays original Audubon watercolors, Early American toys, Tiffany lamps, antique vehicles, and Hudson River School landscapes. There is an important research library on the second floor. *170 Central Park West at 77th St., tel. 212/873–3400. Admission: $3 adults, $2 senior citizens, $1 children under 12; pay what you wish Tues. Open Tues.–Sun. 10–5.*

4 The **American Museum of Natural History,** the adjacent **Hayden Planetarium,** and the surrounding grounds take up a four-block tract bounded by Central Park West, Columbus Avenue, and 77th and 81st streets. With a collection of more than 36 million items, the museum certainly has something for every taste, from a 94-foot blue whale to the 563-carat Star of India sapphire. The Naturemax Theater projects films on a giant screen. The Hayden Planetari-

um (on 81st Street) has two stories of exhibits, and several different Sky Shows projected on 22 wraparound screens. The rock Laser Shows draw crowds of teenagers on Friday and Saturday nights. *Museum: tel. 212/769–5100. Suggested contribution: $5 adults, $2.50 children. Open Sun.–Tues. and Thurs. 10–5:45; Wed., Fri., and Sat. 10–9. Planetarium: tel. 212/769 5920. Admission: $4 adults; $3 senior citizens, members, and students; $2 children; $7 for laser show. Open weekdays 12:30–4:45, Sat. 10–5:45, Sun. noon–5:45. Naturemax Theater admission: $5–$7 adults, $2.50–$3.50 children.*

Upper Broadway

Another Upper West Side trail angles diagonally from Columbus Circle up Broadway. At the world headquarters of the **American Bible Society** (1865 Broadway at 61st St.), you ascend a ruby-red carpet to a little-known second-floor museum that has temporary exhibits of the society's worldwide Bible-distributing activities and permanent displays of Helen Keller's 10-volume Braille Bible, a replica of the original Gutenberg press, and a Torah (Jewish scriptures) from China. An adjunct to Lincoln Center, **The Ballet Shop** (1887 Broadway at 62nd St.) sells books and records, photos, paraphernalia, and mementos.

5 Covering an eight-block area west of Broadway between 62nd and 66th streets, **Lincoln Center** is an architecturally unified group of buildings that houses New York's major-league performing arts institutions. Built during the 1960s to supplant a rundown urban ghetto, the complex can at one time seat nearly 15,000 spectators for performances of classical music, opera, ballet, drama, and film.

Lincoln Center consists of eight distinct units. **Avery Fisher Hall,** named after the founder of Fisher Radio, hosts the New York Philharmonic Orchestra. The Metropolitan Opera and American Ballet Theatre perform at the **Metropolitan Opera House.** The **New York State Theater** is home to the New York City Ballet and the New York City Opera. The **Guggenheim Bandshell,** south of the Met, has free open-air concerts in summer. A single structure devoted to drama includes the **Vivian Beaumont** and **Mitzi E. New-**

house theaters. The **Library and Museum of the Performing Arts** maintains an extensive collection of records, scores, and books on music, theater, and dance. Across 65th Street lies the world-renowned **Juilliard School,** which houses **Alice Tully Hall,** home of the Chamber Music Society of Lincoln Center and the New York Film Festival Center.

Visitors can wander freely through the lobbies of all buildings and relax in Damrosch Park or beside Lincoln Center's fountains; an outdoor cafe operates throughout the summer. The best free indoor attractions are found in the Performing Arts Library, where visitors can listen to a collection of 42,000 records and tapes or check out any of four galleries. A one-hour guided "Take-the-Tour" covers all the grand theaters. *Tel. 212/877–1800, ext. 512, for schedule. Admission: $6.75 adults, $5.75 students and senior citizens, $3.75 children.*

Tickets for Lincoln Center events are costly and, because many performances sell out to season subscribers, sometimes impossible to obtain at box offices or through ticket services. Some tickets are usually available just outside the theater during the half-hour before the performance, someone's companion(s) having been unable to make it. Occasionally there are scalpers, and although it's illegal in New York to sell tickets for more than a specified amount above the printed price, such commerce transpires more or less openly before every performance.

Across the busy intersection from Lincoln Cen-
6 ter, the long-orphaned **Museum of American
Folk Art** has found a new home at Columbus Avenue and 66th Street. Its collection includes Naive paintings, quilts, carvings, dolls, trade signs, painted wooden carousel horses, and a giant Indian-chief copper weathervane. *2 Lincoln Sq., tel. 212/977–7298. Admission free. Open daily 9–9.*

One of the busiest spots on the Upper West Side is the intersection of Broadway, Amsterdam Avenue, and 72nd Street. Officially, the area south of 72nd Street is **Sherman Square** (for the Union Civil War general, William Tecumseh)
7 and the area north of 72nd Street is **Verdi Square**

(for the Italian composer, Giuseppe). In the '70s, Verdi Square was an addicts' hangout known informally as Needle Park. The Upper West Side in general and this intersection in particular have improved considerably in recent years, and real estate values have had a dramatic upsurge.

The **subway kiosk** on the island south of 72nd Street is an official city landmark, a structure with rounded neo-Dutch moldings that was the first express station north of 42nd Street. Occupying the southeast corner of Amsterdam Avenue and 72nd Street is **Gray's Papaya,** a New York quasi-institution that pairs the sacred (health-enriching papaya and other natural juices) with the profane (hot dogs, smothered in sauerkraut and onions if desired).

Farther up Broadway are two of New York's great food shrines. The fresh produce in the bountiful but unpretentious **Fairway Market** (2127 Broadway at 74th St.) practically bursts onto the street. Have a look at the handmade signs describing the produce and cheese; they can be as fresh as the merchandise itself. At Broadway and 80th Street, **Zabar's** sells exquisite delicatessen items, prepared foods, gourmet groceries, coffees, and cheeses. A mezzanine level has cookware, dishes, and small appliances. The prices are competitive.

When the **Ansonia Hotel** opened at Broadway and 73rd Street in 1904, its white facade, fairy-castle turrets, and new soundproof walls attracted show people and writers to a hitherto unfashionable area. Now an apartment building, the Ansonia has provided temporary homes for Florenz Ziegfeld, Mischa Elman, Theodore Dreiser, and the great Babe Ruth.

For a quick off-Broadway experience, walk two
8 blocks west to the **Soldiers and Sailors Monument** at Riverside Drive and 89th Street. The monument commemorates Civil War casualties; the environs afford a refreshing view of Riverside Park, the lazy Hudson River, and the New Jersey shore.

Pomander Walk is an attractive slice of Old England wedged between 94th and 95th streets,

between Broadway and West End Avenue. The charming enclave was inspired by the stage sets of an American version of a British play of 1911, *Pomander Walk*. Walk in—or peep through the gate if it's locked—and see Tudor houses, window boxes, and neatly trimmed hedges. Around
9 the corner, **Symphony Space,** a not-for-profit, community-sponsored center for the performing arts, presents a regular schedule of low-priced (free–$20) classical, international, and contemporary concerts, readings, and assorted marathons (Mozart, James Joyce, Cole Porter). *2537 Broadway at 95th St., tel. 212/864–5400.*

10 The **Cathedral of St. John the Divine,** one block east of Broadway, is New York's major Episcopal church and the largest Gothic cathedral in the world (St. Peter's Basilica in Rome is the largest church of any kind). The vast 600-foot nave can seat 5,000 worshipers. Small, uniquely outfitted chapels border the nave, and a "Biblical Garden" contains herbs and flowers mentioned in the Bible. It's still perhaps 100 years from completion, and master craftsmen are instructing neighborhood youth in the traditional methods of stonecutting and carving. Along with Sunday services (8, 9, 9:30 [in Spanish]), and 11 AM, and 7 PM), the cathedral operates community outreach programs and presents nonreligious (classical, folk, winter solstice) concerts. *Amsterdam Ave. at 112th St., tel. 212/316–7400, box office 212/662–2133. Tours Mon.–Sat. 11, Sun. 12:45.*

11 The main campus of **Columbia University** (founded 1754), a large and wealthy private institution, occupies an area bounded by 114th and 121st streets, Broadway, and Amsterdam Avenue. Enter from either direction on 116th Street: The buildings so effectively wall off the city that it's easy to believe you've been transported to a more rustic Ivy League campus. The central campus has the rotunda-topped Low Memorial Library to the north and the massive Butler Library to the south. A cafe on the southwest corner of the quad has indoor and outdoor tables perfectly situated for student-watching.

East of the Columbia campus and a short block farther east of Amsterdam Avenue, Morningside Drive runs along a ridge that lies above the incline of Morningside Park and affords an impressive view of the low-rise buildings of Harlem that stretch across the city.

12 **Riverside Church** (Riverside Dr. at 122nd St., tel. 212/222–5900) is nondenominational, interracial, international, extremely political, and socially conscious. It is a massive structure with a 356-foot observation tower (admission: $1) and a 74-bell carillon, the largest in the world, whose bells range in weight from 10 pounds to 20 tons. Along with regular Sunday services (10:45 AM), community events, concerts, and dance and theater programs abound. A reasonably priced, reasonably good cafeteria operates on weekdays and Sundays. *Open daily 9–5.*

Across Riverside Drive, in Riverside Park, stands the General Grant National Memorial
13 Monument, commonly known as **Grant's Tomb,** where the Civil War general and two-term president and his wife rest. In addition to the sarcophagi, the white granite mausoleum contains photographs and Grant memorabilia. *Riverside Dr. at 122nd St., tel. 212/666–1640. Admission free. Open Wed.–Sun. 9–5.*

Tour 7: Upper East Side

Numbers in the margin correspond with points of interest on the Upper East Side map.

The Upper East Side is the area east of Central Park between 60th and 96th streets. Long the city's most expensive and desirable residential area, the Upper East Side is the home of old money, new money, foreign money—any kind of money will do. From Fifth Avenue mansions and the smart town houses of the East 60s and 70s to the high-rise corridors of First and Second avenues, this area, more than any other, epitomizes what many people think of as the Manhattan style.

Begin a tour of the Upper East Side at the Plaza.
1 That can mean either **Grand Army Plaza,** an open space along Fifth Avenue between 58th and 60th streets, or the world-famous hotel at the western border of that space. Shaped like the token for a hotel in Monopoly, the **Plaza Ho-**

Central Park Zoo, **5**
Frick Collection, **7**
Grand Army Plaza, **1**
Great Lawn, **4**
Guggenheim Museum, **11**
International Center of Photography, **14**
Jewish Museum, **13**
Loeb Boathouse, **3**
Metropolitan Museum of Art, **10**
El Museo del Barrio, **16**
Museum of the City of New York, **15**
National Academy of Design, **12**
Ralph Lauren, **8**
Temple Emanu-El, **6**
Whitney Museum, **9**
Wollman Rink, **2**

Upper East Side

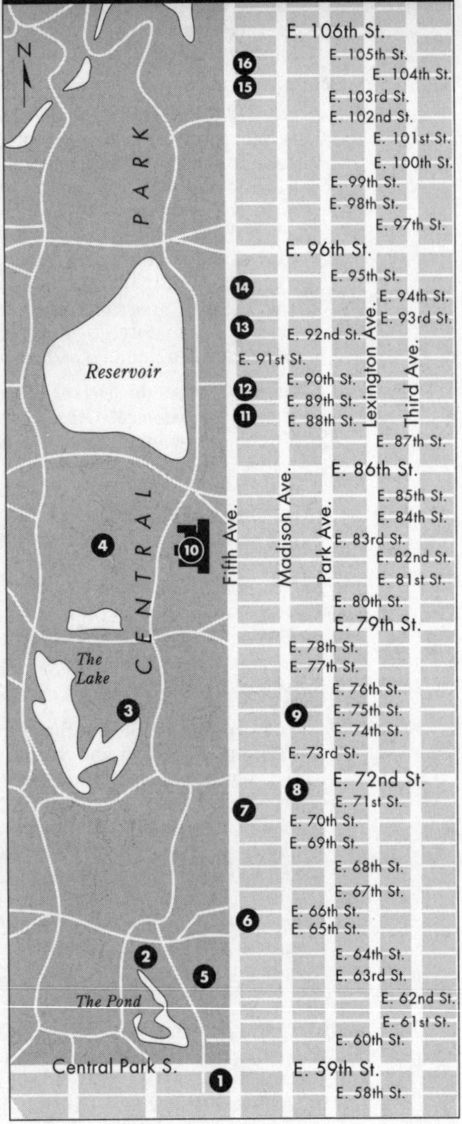

tel is a registered historical landmark that has been in fashion for upper-crust transients, charity balls, coming-out parties, and romantic rendezvous since 1907.

Grand Army Plaza is flanked by a gilded equestrian statue of William Tecumseh Sherman on the north and the Pulitzer (of Pulitzer Prize fame) Fountain to the south. Appropriately enough for this ritzy area, the fountain is crowned by a female figure representing Abundance. When the fountain is dry (as it is much of the time), its rims become perches for sunbathers and the clients of food vendors who station themselves along the perimeter of the plaza.

Grand Army Plaza, or most intersections of Central Park South, is the place to look for horse-drawn carriage rides through the park. Like motorized taxi drivers, hansom drivers are independent operators, and the quality of your ride will depend much on their disposition. Carriages operate all year, except in extremely hot or cold weather, and blankets are provided when it's cool. The city sets the official rates ($34 for the first 20 minutes, $10 for each additional 15 minutes), but drivers will often try to get more. Be sure to agree on a price in advance.

Adjacent to Grand Army Plaza stands the **General Motors Building,** an imposing 50-story Georgia marble tower. One section of the main floor lobby displays a dozen or so shining new GM vehicles. The other part of the lobby has recently become the flagship of the legendary **F.A.O. Schwarz** toy store. Bigger than it looks from outside, the toy-o-rama extends up and around the south side of the GM building, all the way over to the Madison Avenue side. A vast selection, good lighting, and gorgeous displays make this a pleasant place to shop—and somewhat compensate for the lofty price tags. The store contains a Hair Parlour for teenage cuts and a Two-Minute Shop where people pressed for time can choose from a selection of wrapped and ready toys.

Central Park Central Park is the 843-acre space bounded by 59th Street and 110th Street, Fifth Avenue and Central Park West (Eighth Avenue). Spared from the schemes of real estate developers by a

New York Evening Post campaign that began in 1850, Central Park was designed by Frederick Law Olmsted and Calvert Vaux and constructed by a crew of 3,000 mainly Irish workmen and 400 horses.

Today Central Park hosts just about any activity a city dweller might engage in out of doors: jogging, cycling, horseback riding, softball, ice skating, croquet, tennis, bird-watching, boating, chess, checkers, theater, concerts, skateboarding, and break dancing. Central Park is reasonably safe during the day, though the frightening attack on a jogger in 1989 has reminded New Yorkers to stay out of it at night. *Tel. 212/397–3156 for general information, 212/360–1333 for a recorded message on city park events, 212/427–4040 for information on weekend walks and talks led by Urban Park Rangers. Bus tours are offered on Tues. and Thurs.*

East Drive is the road that runs north through Central Park from Grand Army Plaza; like West Drive, the southbound artery in the western precincts of the park, it is closed to automobiles on weekends and during some hours on weekdays. Strolling north along East Drive, you soon pass the buildings of the newly renovated Central Park Zoo, which must be entered from the Fifth Avenue side, at 64th Street.

Beyond the zoo, East Drive takes you past the
2 **Wollman Rink** (tel. 212/517–4800), an ice-skating rink that has become a symbol of contemporary urban life. Fruitless and costly attempts by the city to repair the deteriorated facility had kept the rink closed for years, until the builder Donald Trump adopted the project and quickly completed it. In the minds of New Yorkers, the Wollman Rink represents municipal incompetence conquered by the efficiency of private enterprise.

East Drive loops around to **The Mall,** a broad walkway lined with stately elms and busts of famous men. Here one is likely to witness whatever new craze has come along, from the latest dance to some trendy Oriental athletic discipline. The Mall leads to the **Bandshell,** site of summer concerts, speeches, and performance art. A bit farther north, the handsome, newly renovated **Bethesda Fountain** and the graceful iron bridge often model for "Sunday in New York" postcard pictures.

3 At the **Loeb Boathouse** you can rent a rowboat to cruise the lake or a bike for a spin around the park. You can also buy a fast-food snack or a sit-down lunch. North of the lake is the **Ramble,** a wooded, hilly area scored by twisting paths, where bird-watchers gather early in the morning, especially during the migratory seasons.

As East Drive moves into the 80s, it passes between the sprawling Metropolitan Museum of Art (on the right) and the eastern edge of the
4 **Great Lawn** (about 50 yards to the left). The athletic fields of the Great Lawn are busy most summer evenings and on weekends, and its wide expanse has accommodated tens of thousands of people for megaconcerts by Luciano Pavarotti, Diana Ross, Simon and Garfunkel, and others. Should you see a few hundred people picnicking on the ground in an orderly formation that extends around the oval edge of the lawn, you'll know it's summer and there's a performance that night at the nearby **Delacorte Theater** of the New York Shakespeare Festival. *Tel. 212/598–7100. Admission free. Tickets distributed at 6:15 PM for the performance at 8 PM.*

Fifth Avenue Upper Fifth Avenue was settled during the last decade of the 19th century by millionaire migrants from the 34th Street area, the Astors, the Carnegies, the Vanderbilts, and the Whitneys, who moved into palatial stone mansions overlooking newly fashionable Central Park. Few of the residential mansions remain. Some were supplanted by high-rise apartments, others were transformed into museums or foundation headquarters. The west side of Fifth Avenue is one of the few city walks where intersections will not constantly interrupt your stroll.

Fifth Avenue above Grand Army Plaza begins on a literary note, with **open-air bookstalls** operated (when the weather is reasonably clement) by the Strand and Rogers & Cogswell bookstores. The stalls sell new and used books, New York maps and reference material, cassette tapes, and postcards. The best buys are the half-price "reviewers copies" of lightly used recent hardcover books and brand new trade paperbacks.

A few blocks north, at 64th Street, the **Arsenal Building** stands before the entrance to New York City's newest attraction, the 5.5-acre
5 **Central Park Zoo.** Reopened in August 1988 following a five-year, $35 million renovation, the wildlife showcase re-creates a series of habitats that include polar, temperate, and tropical climate zones in which animals roam at will. Visitors look on from various vantage points in each habitat and can even watch the animals' underwater activities. Polar bears and penguins are among the attractions; there are no elephants here. Admission to the adjacent children's zoo, which at press time was closed for renovations, is granted to adults only when accompanied by a child. *Central Park at E. 64th St., tel. 212/439–6500. Admission: $2.50 adults, 50¢ children 3–12, $1.25 senior citizens. Open Apr.–Oct., weekdays 10–4:30 (May–Sept., Tues. 10–7) weekends and holidays 10–5; Nov.–Mar., daily 10–4. Children under 16 not admitted without an adult.*

6 With seats for 2,500 worshippers, **Temple Emanu-El** (1929) is the world's largest Reform Jewish synagogue. Built in 1929 of limestone, it is covered with mosaics and designed in the Romanesque style with Byzantine influences; the building features Moorish and Art Deco ornamentation. *Fifth Ave. at 65th St., tel. 212/744–1400. Services Mon.–Thurs. 5:30 PM; Fri. 5:15 PM; Sat. 10:30 AM. Guided group tours by appointment only.*

7 The **Frick Collection** is housed in the mansion built by the Pittsburgh coke and steel baron Henry Clay Frick. It was designed to display his private collection of art, and a bona fide masterpiece graces almost every room: Rembrandt's *The Polish Rider*, Fragonard's series *The Progress of Love*, Jan Van Eyck's *Virgin and Child with Saints and Donor*, and distinguished works by Bellini, Vermeer, Titian, El Greco, Turner, Whistler, and Gainsborough. Even the rest area is a masterpiece: a tranquil indoor court with a fountain and glass ceiling. *1*

E. 70th St., tel. 212/288–0700. Admission: $3 adults, $1.50 students and senior citizens. Open Tues.–Sat. 10–6, Sun. 1–6, closed holidays.

The Madison Mile Just before World War I, the railroad tracks down the center of Park Avenue were covered with a roadway, and Park Avenue, like Fifth Avenue, became a distinguished residential thoroughfare. Between the two avenues, the low-rise brownstones of Madison Avenue, which had started out as a commercial universe serving the grand mansions of Fifth Avenue, remain unchanged.

The connotation of "Madison Avenue" has undergone a major change in recent years. New Yorkers no longer readily associate the words (or the place) with the advertising business, much of which has fled Madison Avenue in the East 40s and 50s for less costly downtown real estate. Madison Avenue, in particular the Madison Mile between 59th and 79th streets, is now the home of high chic: The lower stories of Madison Avenue's brownstones house many of the world's major fashion designers, patrician art galleries, and unique specialty stores. For the most part, these shops are small, intimate, expensive, and almost invariably closed on Sunday.

Heading uptown and working both sides of the street, you come to **The Coach Store** (710 Madison Ave.), which devotes two floors to fine leather. **M. J. Knoud** (716 Madison Ave.) purveys hunting and polo saddles and accessories, jockey silks, and other equine-themed clothing and gear.

As opulent as the boudoirs for which its wares are destined, **La Lingerie** (792 Madison Ave.) features high-priced nightgowns, dressing gowns, embroidered shawls, and other intimate apparel. At the same address, **Sonia Rykiel** sells expensive high-fashion garments in styles that won't go out of style next month.

Once owned by the former New York Yankees manager, **Billy Martin's Western Wear** (812 Madison Ave.) features urbane renderings of city-slicker saddlebags, cowboy shirts, suede jackets, Indian-style silver, beaded jewelry, and snakeskin-brimmed baseball caps for all the major league teams. A familiar name in European high fashion, **Giorgio Armani** (815 Madison Ave.) is a "soft-tech" setting for men's and women's clothing in Armani-made and licensed lines. One of the first Madison Mile designer boutiques, **St. Laurent Rive-Gauche** (855 Madison Ave.) is a somewhat haughty place to shop for women's fashions, accessories, and cosmetics.

8 By far the most spectacular store on Madison Mile, **Ralph Lauren** (867 Madison Ave.) hardly seems like a store at all. In fact, it's the landmark Rhinelander Mansion replete with walnut fittings, Oriental carpets, family portraits, and all that high-style preppie clothing that seems to be lying around waiting to be put away. The atmosphere surpasses unintimidating; it's actually inviting. Be sure to visit the fourth-floor home furnishings section, where merchandise is arrayed in to-the-manor-born dream suites.

One Night Stand (905 Madison Ave., tel. 212/772–7720) *rents* designer ball gowns and cocktail dresses; call for an appointment. **Antiquariun Fine Ancient Arts Gallery** (948 Madison Ave.) is a small gallery that specializes in fine ancient art.

9 The **Whitney Museum of American Art** is a gray granite vault separated from Madison Avenue materialism by a dry moat. An outgrowth of a gallery that began in the studio of the sculptor and collector Gertrude Vanderbilt Whitney, the museum is devoted exclusively to 20th-century American work, from naturalism and impressionism to pop art, abstractionism, and whatever comes next. *945 Madison Ave. at 75th St., tel. 212/570–3676. Admission: $5 adults, $3 senior citizens; free for students with school I.D. and children at all times and for everyone Tues. 6–8. Open Tues. 1–8, Wed.–Sat. 11–5, Sun. noon–6.*

Just off Madison is the so-called **Gucci Townhouse** (16 E. 76th St.), the former Gucci family mansion, which in 1988 sold for $7 million, at the time the most ever paid for a New York town house.

Time Out Stop in at the homey, casual **Kalinka Cafe** (1067 Madison at 81st St., tel. 212/472–9656) for a bit of borscht or some chicken Kiev. This narrow restaurant features fresh flowers and delicious Russian entrées ranging from $9 to $20.

Continue north on Madison to the **Frank E. Campbell Funeral Chapel** (1076 Madison Ave. at 81st St.), *the* place for fashionable funerals since 1898. The somber chocolate-color edifice has seen massive funeral events for Rudolph Valentino (1926) and Judy Garland (1969) and more recent ceremonies for Robert Kennedy, John Lennon, and Rita Hayworth. Across the street you may recognize P.S. 6 as Justin Henry's school in *Kramer v. Kramer*.

Museum Mile Museum Mile is a strip of cultural institutions located on or near Fifth Avenue between 82nd and 104th streets, including some of New York's most famous museums.

⑩ The **Metropolitan Museum of Art** has valid evidence for billing itself "New York's number one tourist attraction." This is the largest art museum in the Western Hemisphere (1.6 million square feet), and its permanent collection of some 3 million works of art includes items from prehistoric to modern times from all areas of the world. Its 19 curatorial departments include the world's most comprehensive collection of American art, and its holdings of European art are unequaled outside Europe. The museum also has one of the world's best collections of ancient Greek, Roman, and Egyptian art.

Within this "city of art," New Yorkers tend to prefer the old neighborhoods. The small chamber lined with reliefs from the Northwest Palace of the Assyrian King Assurnasirpal II (BC 882–859) replicates the serene atmosphere of an undiscovered tomb. The Astor Court Chinese garden reproduces a Ming Dynasty (1368–1644) scholar's courtyard with water splashing over artfully positioned rocks. The magnificent Temple of Dendur (circa BC 15) was transplanted from Egypt to a huge gallery with a wall of windows looking onto Central Park.

Walking tours and lectures are free with your admission contribution. Tours covering various sections of the museum begin about every 15 minutes on weekdays, less frequently on weekends. They depart from the Tour Board in the Great Hall (main entrance), but you may attach yourself to any group you encounter along the way. Lectures, which are often related to temporary exhibitions, are given frequently. On Friday and Saturday evenings, New Yorkers gather here to tour the galleries or just relax on the balcony while listening to the string quartet and sipping wine by candlelight. *Fifth Ave. at 82nd St., tel. 212/535–7710. Suggested contribution: $6 adults, $3 senior citizens and students, children free. Open Fri. and Sat. 9:30–8:45, Tues.–Thurs. and Sun. 9:30–5:15.*

11 Frank Lloyd Wright's **Guggenheim Museum** is a six-story spiral rotunda through which you wind down past mobiles, stabiles, and other exemplars of modern art. Displays alternate new artists and modern masters; the permanent collection includes more than 20 Picassos. A newly expanded and fully restored Guggenheim Museum reopened in the fall of 1991 after being closed for a half-year. A new tower and expanded gallery space display the newly acquired Panza Collection of Minimalist art, among other works. *1071 Fifth Ave. at 89th St., tel. 212/360–3513. Admission: $4.50 adults, $2.50 students and senior citizens, free Tues. 5–7:45. Open Tues. 11–7:45, Wed.–Sun. 11–4:45.*

Housed in a stately 19th-century mansion, the
12 exhibitions of **The National Academy of Design** usually focus on comparatively unsung artists of Europe and America. *1083 Fifth Ave. at 89th St., tel. 212/369–4880. Admission: $3.50 adults, $2 senior citizens and students, free Tues. 5–8. Open Tues. noon–8, Wed.–Sun. noon–5.*

A former residence of the industrialist and philanthropist Andrew Carnegie now houses the **Cooper-Hewitt Museum,** officially the Smithsonian Institution's National Museum of Design. Exhibitions, which change regularly, focus on an aspect of contemporary or historical design. Major holdings include: drawings, prints, textiles, furniture, metalwork, ceramics, glass, woodwork, and wall coverings. *2 E. 91st St., tel. 212/860–6868. Admission: $3 adults, $1.50 senior citizens and students, free Tues. 5–9. Open Tues. 10–9, Wed.–Sat. 10–5, Sun. noon–5.*

Time Out **Jackson Hole** (Madison Ave. at 91st St.) is a cheerful spot that serves the great American hamburger, sandwiches, omelets, chicken, and salads. Ski posters evoke the mood of the eponymous Wyoming resort. Prices are reasonable; beer is available.

13 The largest collection of Jewish ceremonial objects in the Western Hemisphere is usually housed in the **Jewish Museum.** The museum is closed for renovation through 1992, during which time it will present its exhibitions at the New-York Historical Society (*see* Tour 6, above). *1109 Fifth Ave. at 92nd St., tel. 212/399–3344.*

14 Located in a landmark mansion at the corner of Fifth Avenue and 94th Street, the **International Center of Photography** (ICP) generally focuses its exhibitions on the work of a single prominent photographer or one photographic genre. The bookstore carries an impressive array of photography-oriented books, prints, and postcards; courses and special programs are offered throughout the year. *1130 Fifth Ave., tel. 212/860–1777. Admission: $3 adults, $1.50 students, $1 senior citizens and children under 12, free Tues. 5–8. Open Tues. noon–8, Wed.–Fri. noon–5, Sat.–Sun. 11–6.*

15 The **Museum of the City of New York** makes the history of the Big Apple—from the Dutch settlers of Nieuw Amsterdam to yesterday's headlines—come to life with period rooms, dioramas, slide shows, and clever displays of memorabilia. Weekend programs appeal especially to children. *Fifth Ave. at 103rd St., tel. 212/534–1672. Suggested contribution: $4 adults, $2 students, senior citizens, and $1 children. Open Tues.–Sat. 10–5; Sun. and legal holidays, 1–5.*

16 The final stop on Museum Mile, **El Museo del Barrio,** concentrates on Latin culture in general, with a particular emphasis on Puerto Rican

art. The permanent collection includes numerous pre-Columbian artifacts. *1230 Fifth Ave. at 104th St., tel. 212/831–7272. Suggested contribution: $2. Open Wed.–Sun. 11–5.*

Tour 8: Greenwich Village

Numbers in the margin correspond with points of interest on the Greenwich Village and the East Village map.

Writers and artists have converged on Greenwich Village for generations. In the 19th century the writers Henry James, Edgar Allan Poe, Mark Twain, Walt Whitman, and Stephen Crane lived and worked in the area. The turn of the century brought O. Henry, Edith Wharton, Theodore Dreiser, and Hart Crane. During the 1920s and 1930s, John Dos Passos, Norman Rockwell, Sinclair Lewis, Eugene O'Neill, Edward Hopper, and Edna St. Vincent Millay resided in its row houses and frequented its speakeasies.

During the late 1940s and early 1950s, Village cultural life was dominated by the Abstract Expressionist painters Franz Kline, Jackson Pollock, Mark Rothko, and Willem de Kooning and the beat writers Jack Kerouac, Allen Ginsberg, and Lawrence Ferlinghetti. A later wave brought the folk musicians and poets of the 1960s, led by Bob Dylan and Peter, Paul, and Mary.

As in much of Manhattan, high rents have priced all but the most affluent out of the Greenwich Village housing market. Today the Village—New Yorkers almost invariably speak of it simply as "the Village"—is inhabited principally by affluent professionals, students, and others aspiring to blend the flavor of small-town life with the bright lights of the big city.

Begin a tour of Greenwich Village at Washington
1 ton Arch in **Washington Square** at the foot of Fifth Avenue. Designed by Stanford White, Washington Arch was built in 1892 to commemorate the 100th anniversary of George Washington's presidential inauguration and was originally placed about a half-block north of its

present location. The permanent arch was built in 1906.

Washington Square started out as a cemetery, principally for yellow fever victims, and an estimated 10,000–22,000 bodies lie below. In the early 1800s it was a parade ground and the site of public executions; bodies dangled from a conspicuous Hanging Elm at the northwest corner of the Square. Later it became the focus of a fashionable residential neighborhood and the center of outdoor activity.

By the early 1980s, Washington Square had deteriorated into a tawdry place only a drug dealer could love. Then community activism motivated a police crackdown that sent the drug traffic elsewhere and made Washington Square comfortable again for Frisbee players, street musicians, skateboarders, jugglers, stand-up comics, sitters, strollers, and the twice-a-year art fair.

Most of the buildings bordering Washington Square belong to New York University. **The Row** of federal town houses along Washington Square North, between Fifth Avenue and University Place, serves as faculty housing. The house at 20 Washington Square North is the oldest building (1820) on the block. You can tell it was built before 1830 by the Flemish bond brickwork—alternate bricks inserted with the smaller surface facing out. Before 1830, builders thought that this was the only way to build walls that would stand.

Turn north on MacDougal Street and walk a half-block to **MacDougal Alley,** a private (fenced with locked gate) cobblestone street where stables and carriage houses have been converted into charming homes adorned with gas lamps.

Eighth Street, the main commercial strip of the Village, is not the "real" Greenwich Village but a collection of fast-food purveyors, poster and record shops, and glitzy clothing stores.

Time Out Don't miss **Patisserie Lanciani** (271 W. 4th St., between W. 11th and Perry Sts., tel. 212/929–0739), a tiny black-and-white café where writers

Greenwich Village and the East Village

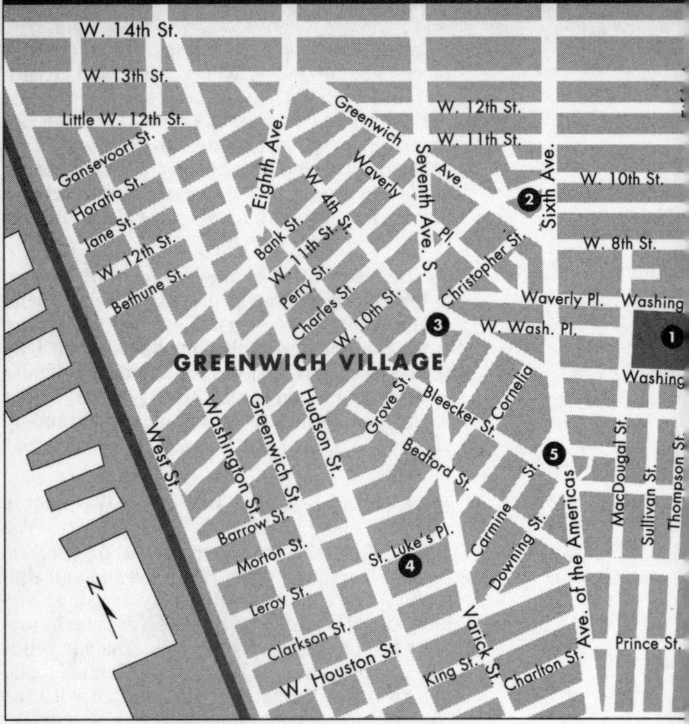

Father Demo Square, **5**
Jefferson Market Library, **2**
Public Theater, **6**
St. Luke's Place, **4**
St. Mark's Church-in-the-Bowery, **7**
St. Mark's Place, **8**
Sheridan Square, **3**
Tompkins Square, **9**
Washington Square, **1**

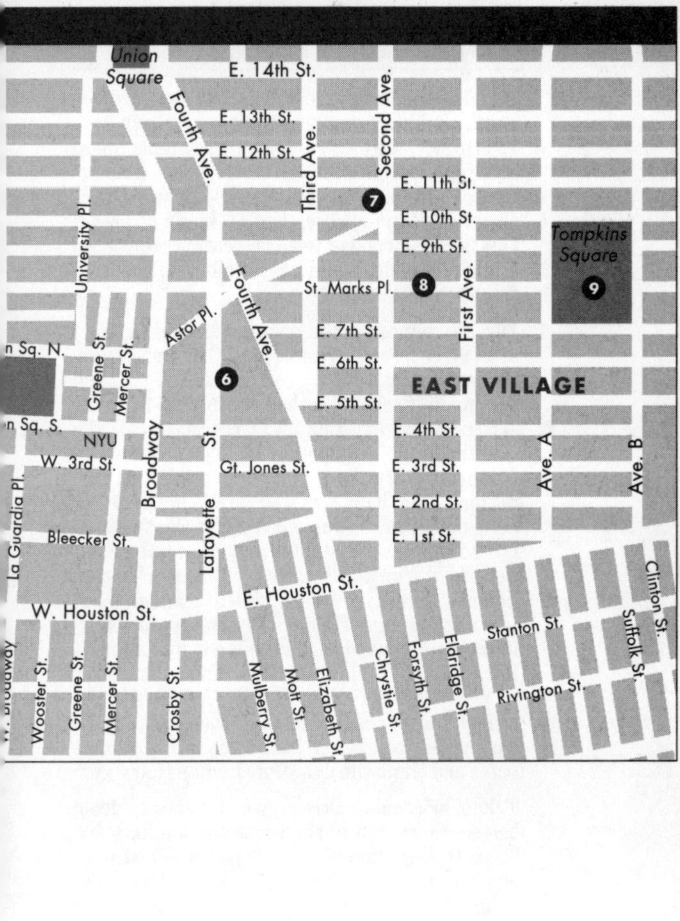
Union Square
E. 14th St.
E. 13th St.
E. 12th St.
Fourth Ave.
Third Ave.
Second Ave.
E. 11th St.
E. 10th St.
E. 9th St.
Tompkins Square
University Pl.
St. Marks Pl.
First Ave.
Astor Pl.
Fourth Ave.
E. 7th St.
E. 6th St.
n Sq. N.
Greene St.
Mercer St.
EAST VILLAGE
E. 5th St.
n Sq. S.
NYU
E. 4th St.
W. 3rd St.
Broadway
St.
Gt. Jones St.
E. 3rd St.
Ave. A
Ave. B
La Guardia Pl.
E. 2nd St.
Lafayette
Bleecker St.
E. 1st St.
E. Houston St.
Clinton St.
W. Houston St.
Stanton St.
Suffolk St.
Wooster St.
Greene St.
Mercer St.
Crosby St.
Mulberry St.
Mott St.
Elizabeth St.
Chrystie St.
Forsyth St.
Eldridge St.
Rivington St.
6
7
8
9

gain inspiration as they sample the fresh-baked pastries and excellent coffee.

For a more authentic village atmosphere, go north on Sixth Avenue to **Balducci's** (Sixth Ave. at 9th St.), a full-service gourmet department store that sprouted from the vegetable stand of the late Louis Balducci, Sr. Along with more than 80 Italian cheeses and 50 kinds of bread, this family-owned enterprise features imported Italian specialties and a prodigious selection of fresh seafood.

Directly opposite, the triangle formed by West 10th Street, Sixth Avenue, and Greenwich Avenue originally held a greenmarket, a jail, and the magnificent courthouse that is now the
2 **Jefferson Market Library.** Critics termed the courthouse's hodgepodge of styles Venetian, Victorian, or Italian; Villagers, noting the alternating wide bands of red brick and narrow strips of granite, dubbed it Lean Bacon style. Over the years the structure has housed a number of government agencies (public works, civil defense, census bureau, police academy) but was on the verge of demolition when public-spirited citizens saved it and turned it into a public library in 1967. Note the fountain at the corner of West 10th Street and Sixth Avenue and the seal of the City of New York on the east front; on the inside, look at the handsome interior doorways and climb the graceful circular stairway.

Take Christopher Street, which veers off from the southern end of the library triangle, a few steps to **Gay Street.** A bending lane lined with small row houses circa 1810, Gay Street was originally a black neighborhood and later a strip of speakeasies. Ruth McKinney lived and wrote *My Sister Eileen* in the basement of No. 14, and Howdy Doody was designed in the basement of No. 12.

Go west on Christopher past the **Lion's Head** (59 Christopher St.), a longtime hangout for literati.

3 At **Sheridan Square,** Christopher Street becomes the heart of New York's gay community and the location of many intriguing boutiques.

West of Seventh Avenue, the Village turns into a picture-book town of twisting, tree-lined streets, quaint houses, and tiny restaurants. Follow Grove Street from Sheridan Square past the boyhood home of the poet Hart Crane (45 Grove St.) to the house at the corner of Grove and Bedford streets. This building merits notice as one of the few clapboard structures in the Village; wood construction was banned as a fire hazard in 1822, the year it was built. The house has served many functions; it housed a brothel during the Civil War.

Grove Street curves before the iron gate of **Grove Court,** an enclave of brick-fronted town houses of the middle 1800s. Built originally as apartments for employees at neighborhood hotels, Grove Court was called Mixed Ale Alley because of the residents' propensity to pool beverages brought from work. It now houses a more affluent crowd: A town house there recently sold for $3 million.

Time Out Where Christopher meets Grove Street and Waverly Place, **Pierre's** (170 Waverly Pl., tel. 212/929–7194) is everyone's favorite little French corner bistro. The sumptuous couscous and the profiterole are two specialties. Music may include guitar or piano played during dinner at this relaxed, friendly place.

The building at 77 Bedford Street is the oldest house in the Village (1799), yet the place next door has a greater claim to fame. Not only was 75½ Bedford the residence (at different times) of Edna St. Vincent Millay and John Barrymore, it is also New York's narrowest house. Just 9½ feet wide, the lot was an alley until rising real estate prices inspired the construction.

Heading west on Commerce Street, you soon reach the **Cherry Lane Theater,** one of the original Off-Broadway houses and the site of American premieres of works by O'Neill, Beckett, Ionesco, and Albee. Across the street stand two identical brick houses separated by a garden. Popularly known as the **Twin Sisters,** the houses were built (according to legend) by a sea captain for two daughters who loathed each other. Historical records insist they were built by a milkman who needed the two houses and an open courtyard for his work.

Barrow and Hudson streets meet at the corner of a block owned by **St. Luke's-in-the-Fields,** a simple country church whose grounds are made available to church members and neighborhood residents for gardening space.

4 Head south on Hudson Street to **St. Luke's Place,** a row of classic town houses of the 1860s, shaded by graceful ginkgo trees. Mayor Jimmy Walker lived at No. 6. The lampposts are "mayor's lamps," which were sometimes placed in front of the residences of New York mayors. Theodore Dreiser wrote *An American Tragedy* at No. 16. No. 12 is the residence of the Huxtable family depicted in the credits of *The Cosby Show*—but the Huxtables purportedly live in Brooklyn. Before 1890 the playground on the south side of St. Luke's Place was a graveyard where, according to legend, the dauphin of France, the lost son of Louis XVI and Marie Antoinette, is interred.

Across Seventh Avenue, St. Luke's Place becomes Leroy Street, which terminates in an old Italian neighborhood at Bleecker Street. Amazingly unchanged amid all the Village gentrification, Bleecker between Sixth and Seventh avenues abounds with fragrant Italian bakeries (**Zitos,** 259 Bleecker St.), butcher shops (**Ottomanelli's,** 285 Bleecker St.), pastry shops, fish stores, vegetable markets, pizza stands, and restaurants. The activity here focuses on
5 **Father Demo Square** (Bleecker St. and Sixth Ave.). Across Bleecker Street you'll see the **Church of Our Lady of Pompeii,** where Mother Cabrini, the first American saint, often prayed.

Across Sixth Avenue lies the stretch of Bleecker Street depicted in songs by Bob Dylan and other folk singers of the 1960s. Standing in the shadow of New York University, the area around the intersection of Bleecker and MacDougal streets attracts a young crowd to its cafes, bars, jazz clubs, coffeehouses, pizza stands, Off-Broadway theaters (**Provincetown Playhouse, Minetta Lane Theater**), cabarets (**Village Gate**), fast-food stands, and unpretentious restaurants.

Continuing north on MacDougal, you pass two houses (127 MacDougal St. and 129 MacDougal St.) once owned by Aaron Burr, who held much of the land that became Greenwich Village. At the end of the block, you've returned to Washington Square.

Tour 9: The East Village

The gritty tenements of the East Village—an area bounded by 14th Street on the north, Fourth Avenue or the Bowery on the west, Houston Street on the south, and the East River—provided inexpensive living places for artists, writers, and actors until very recently. Now the East Village is as costly a place to live as anywhere else south of 96th Street. Yet, in a way, the area has the best of both worlds. The new residents have been accompanied by new restaurants, shops, and galleries, while the old East Villagers maintain the fascinating trappings of the counterculture.

To explore the East Village, begin at the intersection of East 8th Street, Fourth Avenue, and Astor Place. Works of modern sculpture occupy two traffic islands in the square: One island contains *Alamo*, a massive black cube sculpted by Bernard Rosenthal; another island bears an ornate Beaux Arts subway entrance that provides access to the uptown No. 6 trains. Weather permitting, the sidewalks on the southern edge of Astor Place become a makeshift flea market.

On one corner of the intersection stands **Astor Wine and Spirits** (12 Astor Pl.), one of New York's most comprehensive and attractive liquor stores. It has good prices on imports, even better deals on house brands. (New York State has unexpectedly restrictive liquor control laws: Liquor and wine can be sold only in liquor stores, which can sell *only* liquor and wine—no beer, soda, ice, or glasses—and must close on Sunday.)

Continue west on Astor Place to **Astor Place Hair Designers** (2 Astor Pl.), where lines stretch out to the sidewalk awaiting service by four levels of barbers. Choose your cut from Polaroid snapshots in the window—maybe a Village Cut, a Guido, or a Li'l Tony. It costs only $10 for men and $12 for ladies, and it's open every day.

Returning to Fourth Avenue and heading south on Lafayette Street, you quickly come upon **Colonnade Row.** These run-down row houses of 1833, fronted by marble Corinthian colum, were once inhabited by John Jacob Astor and Cornelius Vanderbilt.

In 1854 Astor opened the city's first free library in the imposing structure directly across the street. That building now houses a significant New York institution, the New York Shake-
6 speare Festival's **Public Theater.** The Public's five playhouses (and a cinema) present plays from abroad, some classic theater, and challenging new work by young American writers. *A Chorus Line* had its first performances here. The New York Shakespeare Festival is in the midst of a six-year Shakespeare marathon that, for the first time in America, will present all 37 plays consecutively. *425 Lafayette St., tel. 212/598–7150. Theater tickets: $10–$25 for regular performances, $30 for Shakespeare marathon productions. Some half-price tickets for most performances available at 6 PM (matinees, 1 PM); the line forms 1–2 hrs earlier, and before that for the most popular shows.*

Cooper Square takes its name from Peter Cooper, an industrialist who in 1859 founded a college to provide a forum for public opinion and free technical education for the working class. The brownstone **Cooper Union Foundation Building** at Astor Place and Fourth Avenue was the first structure to be supported by steel railroad rails—rolled in Cooper's own plant. Cooper Union still offers tuition-free education and an active public-affairs program. Three galleries present changing exhibitions during the academic year.

Old New York joke: Q. How do you get to Carnegie Hall? A. Practice, practice, practice. Variation on old New York joke: Q. How do you get to Carnegie Hall? A. Go to the **Carl Fischer Music Store** (62 Cooper Sq., tel. 212/677–1148), select from the infinitude of sheet music, confer with the knowledgeable staff, mingle with the musicians hanging out there, and practice, practice, practice.

You will probably find **McSorley's Old Ale House** (15 E. 7th St.), one of several claimants to the distinction of being New York's oldest bar, crammed with college types enticed by McSorley's own brands of ale. It opened in 1854 and did not admit women until 1970.

Surma, The Ukrainian Shop (11 E. 7th St.) reminds you that the East Village is essentially a Ukrainian neighborhood of onion-domed churches, butcher shops, bakeries, and restaurants serving hearty Middle European fare. Surma's exotic stock includes Ukrainian books, magazines, and cassette tapes; musical instruments; colorful painted eggs and Surma's own brand of egg coloring; honey; and an exhaustive selection of peasant blouses.

Stuyvesant Street veers away from St. Marks Place and Third Avenue at an angle and runs through what was once Governor Peter Stuyvesant's "bouwerie," or farm. The street
7 ends before **St. Mark's Church-in-the-Bowery,** a fieldstone country church of 1799 appended with a Greek Revival steeple and cast-iron front porch. Stuyvesant and Commodore Perry are buried in the cemetery beside the city's oldest continually used church, which has hosted much countercultural activity over the years. In the 1920s a forward-thinking pastor injected the Episcopalian ritual with American Indian chants, Greek folk dancing, and Eastern mantras. During the hippie era, St. Mark's welcomed avant-garde poets and playwrights. Today, dancers, poets, and performance artists cavort in the main sanctuary, where pews have been removed to accommodate them.

Second Avenue borders the church on the east, a thoroughfare that in the early part of this century was known as the Yiddish Rialto. Between Houston and 14th streets, eight theaters presented Yiddish-language productions of musicals, revues, and heart-wrenching melodramas. Today the theaters are gone; all that remains are Hollywood-style stars that have been embedded in the sidewalk in front of the **Second**

Avenue Deli (Second Ave. and 10th St.) to commemorate the Yiddish stage luminaries.

Time Out For some of the best Italian pastries in the city, try **Veniero Pasticerria** (342 E. 11th St., near 1st Ave., tel. 212/674–7264) a lively café that has rows and rows of incredibly fresh cannolis, fruit tarts, cheesecakes, and other desserts on display. If you can't get in, try **De Robertis Pasticceria** (176 1st Ave., tel. 212/674–7137) across the street; it's a more subdued neighborhood hangout.

8 The intersection of Second Avenue and **St. Marks Place** (the name given to 8th Street in the East Village) is the hub of the "hip" East Village. During the 1950s Allen Ginsberg and Jack Kerouac lived and wrote in the area; the 1960s brought Bill Graham's Fillmore East, the Electric Circus, and hallucinogenic drugs to these blocks. The black-clad, pink-haired or shaven-headed punks followed, and many of them remain today. St. Marks Place between Second and Third avenues is a counterculture bazaar lined with vegetarian restaurants, jewelry stalls, leather shops, haircutters, and stores selling books, posters, and weird clothing. If you want to find a souvenir that will shock Aunt Minnie, this is the place to look. The East Village manages to get all the new styles first; the trend that *Time* magazine will discover in six months is parading St. Marks Place today.

East of Second Avenue, the area becomes more arty. **Theater 80** (80 St. Marks Pl., tel. 212/254–7400), one of New York's few remaining revival movie houses, shows a different double feature almost daily (same show Friday and Saturday); the fare includes American and foreign classics, relatively recent films, and cult classics.

P.S. 122 (150 First Ave. at 9th St., tel. 212/477–5288) is a former public school building transformed into a complex of spaces for avant-garde entertainment. Shocking, often crude, and frequently unpredictable, P.S. 122 happenings translate the spirit of the street into performance art. Prices are low, rarely more than $10, except for occasional benefit performances.

9 Far East Village activities focus on **Tompkins Square,** the park bordered by avenues A and B and 7th and 10th streets. Although the square itself could use a facelift, the restored brownstones along 10th Street are evidence that Tompkins Square is already smartly gentrified.

Not long ago, the outer limits of the East Village were a hotbed of avant-garde activity. More than two dozen art galleries, with names like Gracie Mansion and P.P.O.W., featured work that was often startling, innovative, or political. The art dealers, however, have either gone out of business or moved to more mainstream (and spacious) locations in SoHo or other parts of the Village.

Time Out **Jerry's 103** (103 Second Ave., at Sixth St., tel. 212/777–4120) stays open until 2 AM four days a week, and until 4 AM Thurs.–Sat. Its reasonably priced menu (pizzas, pastas, salads, and seafood) and informal atmosphere make it popular at all hours, especially with young artists.

Tour 10: SoHo

Numbers in the margin correspond with points of interest on the SoHo, Little Italy, and Chinatown map.

Twenty years ago, SoHo (the district South of Houston Street, bounded by Broadway, Canal Street, and Sixth Avenue) had just about been left for dead. In 1962 a City Club of New York study called this area of small 19th-century factories and warehouses "the wasteland of New York City" and "commercial slum number one." Numerous industrial fires had earned it the nickname Hell's Hundred Acres.

Two factors changed the perception and the fate of SoHo. One was the discovery that the hot hundred contained the world's greatest concentration of cast-iron buildings. The architectural rage between 1860 and 1890, cast-iron buildings did not require massive walls to bear the weight of the upper stories. Lighter and less expensive than stone, they were produced from standardized molds to mimic any architectural style: Italianate, Victorian Gothic, and neo-Greek can be seen today in SoHo. By eliminating loadbearing walls, cast-iron buildings gained interior space and made possible larger windows. Many subsequent nonmetallic buildings attempted to copy the graceful cast-iron design; how can you tell true cast-iron buildings from the counterfeits? Hold a magnet against the suspect and see whether it sticks.

The other factor of the SoHo renaissance was the influx of artists attracted to the large, cheap, well-lighted spaces that cast-iron buildings provided. At first it was illegal for artists to live in their lofts; then, during the 1970s, the municipal zoning laws were changed to permit residence. However, as the tide of artists and galleries and quaint cafes made this convenient neighborhood a more attractive residential area, the rising rents forced out all but the most successful artists.

Today, SoHo offers architecture and art, highstyle shopping, and plenty of intriguing places to eat and drink. West Broadway (which runs parallel to and four blocks west of Broadway) is SoHo's main drag and the location of many shops and galleries. Saturday is the big day for gallery-hopping, and it's when the sidewalks of SoHo turn into a strolling fashion show of today's wildest styles.

South on West Broadway from Houston Street (pronounced "How-ston"), **Circle Gallery** (468 West Broadway) spotlights a number of artists at a time and sells posters and jewelry. **Suzanne Bartsch** (456A West Broadway) is a semi-Oriental setting for British-designed clothing. **Victoria Falls** (451 West Broadway) sells authentic antique and reproduced women's clothing, including fine lingerie and handknit sweaters.

1 **420 West Broadway** is one address that houses several galleries: **Leo Castelli Gallery** displays the big names of modern art; **Sonnabend Gallery** has important American and European artists; the **49th Parallel** features Canadian artists; and **Charles Cowles Gallery** has fine painting, sculpture, and photography. Several showrooms in the **Mary Boone Gallery** (417 West Broadway) display what's hot in contemporary art.

It's hard to overlook **Think Big** (390 West Broadway), a shop that features elephantine versions of sporting goods, items commonly found in the home, and souvenirs. Next door, **D. F. Sanders & Co.** (386 West Broadway) markets contemporary furnishings and housewares that look stylish enough to make housework seem like fun. The **O.K. Harris Gallery** (383 West Broadway) is known for works of photorealism and unusual sculpture.

Time Out Head west to find the **TriBeCa Grill** (375 Greenwich St., tel. 212/941–3900). It's located on the first floor of the old Martinson Coffee Building, which now houses actor Robert De Niro's **Tribeca Film Center,** a movie production complex. The Grill specializes in fresh grilled fish, sumptuous salads, and charcuterie. And that's the old Maxwell Plum's bar in the middle of the restaurant.

SoHo's finest cast-iron architecture lies east of West Broadway. Head east on Broome Street and cross Wooster Street, which is paved with Belgian blocks, a smoother successor to the traditional cobblestone. The **Gunther Building,** with its gracefully curving window panes, stands at the southwest corner of Broome and Greene streets. Go north on Greene to #72–76, the so-called **King of Greene Street,** a five-story, Renaissance-style, cast-iron building with a magnificent projecting porch of Corinthian columns. Today the King (now painted yellow) houses art galleries plus **The Second Coming,** a department store of "vintage"—too old for "secondhand," not old enough for "antique"—women's and men's clothing, furniture, and other curiosities. The **Queen of Greene Street** (28–30 Greene St.) is a Second Empire cast-iron structure with a huge mansard roof but no retail enterprises.

Continue east on Broome Street to the corner of Broome and Broadway to see a classic of the
2 cast-iron genre, the 1857 **Haughwout Building** (488 Broadway). Inspired by a Venetian palace, this five-story blackened Parthenon of Cast Iron contained the world's first commercial passenger elevator, a steam-powered device invented

Chatham Square, **8**
420 West Broadway, **1**
Haughwout Building, **2**
Museum of Holography, **4**
New Museum, **3**
New York Chinatown History Project, **7**
Police Building, **5**
Umberto's Clam House, **6**

Soho, Little Italy, and Chinatown

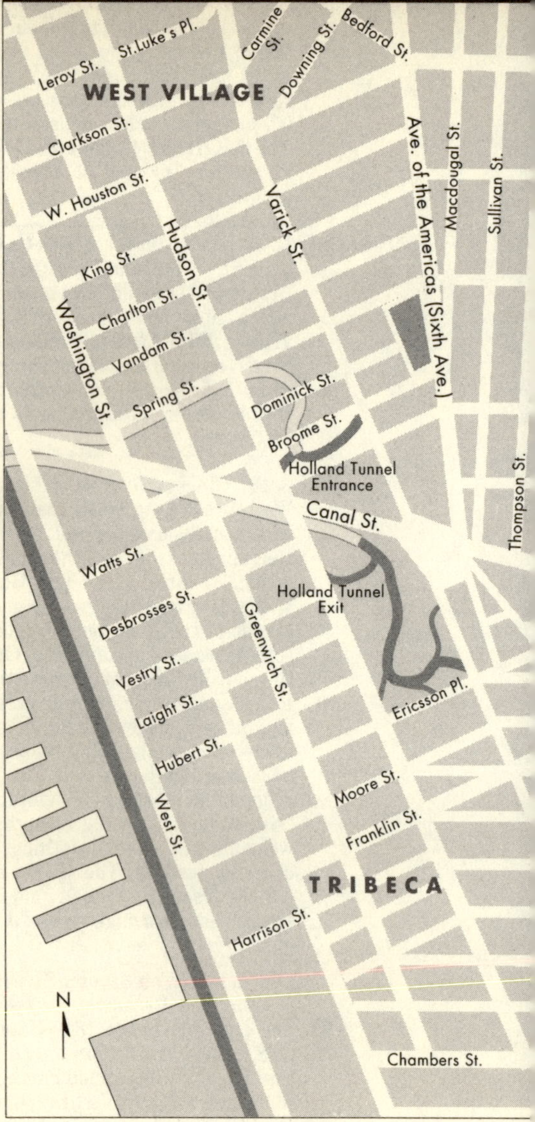

W. Houston St.
E. Houston St.
Lafayette St.
Forsyth St.
Chrystie St.
Prince St.
Mulberry St.
SOHO
Baxter St.
Spring St.
West Broadway
Wooster St.
Greene St.
Mercer St.
Broadway
Crosby St.
Mott St.
Elizabeth St.
Kenmare St.
Bowery
Broome St.
Broome St.
LITTLE ITALY
Grand St.
Lafayette St.
Centre St.
Howard St.
Hester St.
Lispenard St.
Canal St.
West Broadway
Walker St.
Broadway
CHINATOWN
Baxter St.
White St.
Bayard St.
Pell St.
Franklin St.
Doyers St.
Leonard St.
Worth St.
Thomas St.
Pearl St.
Duane St.
Centre St.
Park Row
Reade St.
Church St.
Duane St.
City Hall Park
1
2
3
4
5
6
7
8

by Elisha Graves Otis. For a closer look at the tin ceilings and interior columns, and perhaps a bargain on linens or underwear, step inside the **SoHo Mill Outlet** on the ground floor.

The Broome-Broadway intersection is a few blocks from SoHo's two unusual museums. The
3 **New Museum of Contemporary Art** shows experimental, often radically innovative work by unrecognized artists. It will display nothing more than 10 years old. *583 Broadway between Houston and Prince Sts., tel. 212/219–1222. Suggested admission: $3.50 adults, $2.50 students, senior citizens, and artists. Open Wed., Thurs., and Sun. noon–6; Fri. and Sat. noon–8.*

4 **The Museum of Holography** has a permanent exhibit on the history of holograms, three-dimensional photographs created by laser beams. This combination science show and art gallery projects a film on holography and has three changing exhibitions a year. The gift shop has a terrific selection of 3-D art and souvenirs. *11 Mercer St. (near Canal St.), tel. 212/925–0581. Admission: $3.50 adults, $2.50 students, children, and senior citizens. Open daily 11–6.*

Tour 11: Little Italy

Where are the cops when you need them? Certainly not in the former police headquarters building, a magnificent 1909 Renaissance palazzo that occupies the entire block bounded by Grand, Centre, and Broome streets and Centre Market Place. The police moved to new quarters in 1973, and the stately domed edifice has been converted into a luxury co-op project aptly
5 called the **Police Building,** where apartments range in price from $338,500 to $1,746,000.

Walk one block east to Grand and Mulberry streets, and you enter Little Italy. Look south on Mulberry Street at the tenement buildings with fire escapes projecting over the sidewalks.

Most of these buildings are of the late 19th-century New York tenement style known as railroad flats, six-story buildings on 25-foot by 90-foot lots. The rooms in each apartment are arranged in a straight line, like railroad cars, with no hallway on either side. The style was predominant in the densely populated lower Manhattan until 1901, when the city passed an ordinance requiring air shafts in the interior of buildings.

Mulberry Street has long been the heart of Little Italy, and at this point it's virtually the entire body. In 1932 an estimated 98% of the residents of the area were of Italian birth or heritage; since then the growth and expansion of Chinatown has encroached on the Italian neighborhood to such an extent that the merchants and community leaders of the Little Italy Restoration Association (LIRA) negotiated a truce in which the Chinese agreed to let Mulberry remain an all-Italian street.

Today Mulberry Street between Broome and Canal consists entirely of restaurants, cafes, bakeries, imported food shops, and souvenir stores. Some restaurants and cafes display high-tech Eurodesign; others seem dedicated to remaining precisely as their old customers remember them. How can you find the restaurant that's right for you? Perhaps by choosing the place that displays photos of the celebrity you like best: Sinatra, Cher, Dom DeLuise, Mayor Koch.

Former residents keep returning to Little Italy's venerable institutions. At the corner of Mulberry and Grand, **E. Rossi & Co.** (established 1902) is an antiquated little shop that sells housewares, espresso makers, embroidered religious postcards, and jocular Italian T-shirts. Down the street is **Ferrara's** (195 Grand St.), a 100-year-old pastry shop that ships its creations—cannoli, peasant pie, Italian rum cake—all over the world.

6 **Umberto's Clam House** (129 Mulberry St., tel. 212/431–7545), where mobster Joey Gallo munched his last scungili in 1973, occupies the northwest corner of Mulberry and Hester streets. Quite peaceable now, Umberto's specializes in fresh shellfish in a spicy tomato sauce. Turn onto Hester Street to visit yet another Little Italy institution, **Puglia** (189 Hester St., tel. 212/966–6006), a restaurant where guests sit at long communal tables, sing along with house entertainers, and enjoy moderately priced

southern Italian specialties with quantities of homemade wine.

Around the corner on Baxter Street toward Canal, stands the **San Gennaro Church** (officially, Most Precious Blood Church, National Shrine of San Gennaro), which sponsors Little Italy's annual keynote event, the Feast of San Gennaro. When it happens each September, the streets become a bright and turbulent Italian kitchen.

Tour 12: Chinatown

In theory, Little Italy and Chinatown are divided by Canal Street, the bustling artery that links the Holland Tunnel (to New Jersey) and the Manhattan Bridge (to Brooklyn). However, in recent years Chinatown has gained an influx of immigrants from the People's Republic of China, Taiwan, and especially Hong Kong. Anticipating the return of the British colony to PRC domination in 1997, Hong Kong residents consider Chinatown real estate a safe repository for capital. Consequently, Chinatown has expanded beyond its traditional borders into Little Italy to the north and the formerly Jewish Lower East Side to the east.

Canal Street itself abounds with crowded markets bursting with mounds of fresh seafood and strange-shaped vegetables in extraterrestrial shades of green. Food shops proudly display their wares; if America's motto is "a chicken in every pot," then Chinatown's must be "a roast duck in every window."

The slightly less frantic **Kam Man** (200 Canal St.), a duplex supermarket, has fresh and canned imported groceries, herbs, and the sort of dinnerware and furniture familiar to patrons of Chinese restaurants. Choose from 100 kinds of noodles or such delicacies as dried starch and fresh chicken feet.

Mott Street is the principal business street of the neighborhood. Narrow and twisting; crammed with souvenir shops and restaurants in funky, pagoda-style buildings; crowded with pedestrians at all hours of the day or night, Mott Street looks the way you might expect Chinatown to look. Within the few dense blocks of Chinatown, hundreds of restaurants serve every imaginable type of Chinese cuisine, from simple fast-food noodles or dumplings to sumptuous Hunan, Szechuan, Cantonese, Mandarin, and Shanghai feasts. It may be hard to choose among them, but two things you can know for sure: (1) Every New Yorker thinks he or she knows the absolute flat-out best, and (2) at 8 PM on Saturday, don't be surprised if you have to wait in line to get into any one of them.

In the midst of the Mott Street hubbub stands the **Church of the Transfiguration** (Mott and Mosco Sts.). An imposing Georgian structure built in 1801 as the Zion Episcopal Church, it is now a Chinese Catholic church that delivers mass in Cantonese and Mandarin.

7 The **New York Chinatown History Project** (70 Mulberry St., at the corner of Bayard and Mulberry, tel. 212/619–4785), shows interactive photographic exhibitions on Asian-American labor history. It also has become a resource library and bookstore and offers a walking tour of Chinatown.

Double back to Pell Street, a narrow lane of wall-to-wall restaurants whose neon signs stretch halfway across the thoroughfare. Turn onto **Doyers Street,** a twisty little byway whose storefronts house an extraordinary density of barber shops. Duck into Wing Fat, a new multilevel shopping mall that serpentines its way up, around, and out to Chatham Square.

8 **Chatham Square** is the furthest thing from a square; it's more of a labyrinth, where 10 converging streets create pandemonium for autos and a nightmare for pedestrians. A Chinese arch honoring Chinese casualties in American wars stands on an island in the eye of the storm.

Two remnants of Chinatown's pre-Chinese past stand near Chatham Square. Walk down St. James Place to the **First Shearith Israel graveyard,** the first Jewish cemetery in the United States. When consecrated in 1656, the area was considered outside the city. Walk a half-block farther, turn left on James Street, and you'll see **St. James Church,** a stately 1837 Greek Revival edifice where Al Smith (the former New York governor and a Democratic presidential candidate) served as altar boy.

Go back past Chatham Square and up the Bowery to **Confucius Plaza,** the open area monitored by a statue of Confucius and a high-rise apartment complex named for him. America's oldest drugstore, Olliffe's Apothecary, once occupied an adjacent building at 6 Bowery; now it's the Abacus Federal Savings Bank. At 18 Bowery, corner of Pell Street, stands one of Manhattan's oldest homes, a Federal and Georgian structure built in 1785 by the meat wholesaler Edward Mooney.

Head up the Bowery toward the grand arch and colonnade entrance to the Manhattan Bridge, and you'll soon return to Canal Street. The corner of Bowery and Canal was once the center of New York's diamond district. Many jewelry dealers have moved uptown (to 47th Street between Fifth and Sixth avenues), but a substantial number of jewelers still occupy shops on the Bowery and the north side of Canal. The selection is pretty good, and you shouldn't expect to pay the first price you are quoted.

Tour 13: Lower Manhattan

Numbers in the margin correspond with points of interest on the Lower Manhattan map.

Lower Manhattan is relatively small in area yet dense with attractions. The New Amsterdam colony was established here by the Dutch in 1625, and the first capital of the United States was located in the area. Wall Street is here, which means the New York and American stock exchanges plus innumerable banks and other financial institutions. Boats depart for Staten Island, the Statue of Liberty, and on ferry and excursion routes; the waterfront also inspired the South Street Seaport Museum project.

West Side

1 Our West Side and East Side tours of lower Manhattan both begin outside the **Staten Island Ferry Terminal** at the southernmost tip of Manhattan. For subway riders, that's just outside the South Ferry station on the No. 1 line.

The **Staten Island Ferry** is still the best deal in town. The 20-to-30-minute ride across New

York harbor provides great views of the Manhattan skyline, the Statue of Liberty, the Verrazano Narrows Bridge, and the Jersey coast, and it costs only 50¢ *round-trip*. A word of advice: While commuters love the ferry service's swift new low-slung craft, the boats ride low in the water and have no outside deck space. If one of the low-riders is next in line, you might be happier if you missed the boat and waited for one of the higher, more open old-timers.

To the west of South Ferry lies **Battery Park,** a verdant landfill loaded with monuments and sculpture at Manhattan's green toe. The **East Coast Memorial,** a statue of a fierce eagle, presides over eight granite slabs on which are inscribed the names of U.S. servicemen who died in World War II.

The steps of the East Coast Memorial afford a fine view of the main features of **New York Harbor:** From left to right, **Governor's Island,** a Coast Guard installation; hilly **Staten Island** in the distance; the **Statue of Liberty** on Liberty Island; **Ellis Island,** gateway to the New World for generations of immigrants; and the old railway terminal in **Liberty Park,** on the mainland in Jersey City, New Jersey.

Farther along, you'll see a romantic **statue of Giovanni da Verrazano,** the Florentine merchant who piloted the ship that first sighted New York and its harbor in 1524. From here the Verrazano Narrows Bridge between Brooklyn and Staten Island, the world's longest suspension bridge, is visible beyond Governor's Island.

2 **Castle Clinton** may have gone through more changes than any other public building. Built in 1811 as a defense for New York Harbor, the circular brick fortress was constructed on an island 200 feet from shore. In 1824 it became Castle Garden, an entertainment and concert facility that reached its high point in 1850 when more than 6,000 people (the capacity of Radio City Music Hall) attended the U.S. debut of the "Swedish Nightingale," Jenny Lind. After landfill had connected it to the city, Castle Clinton became, in succession, an immigrant processing center, an aquarium, and now a restored

Bowling Green, **4**
Brooklyn Bridge, **12**
Castle Clinton, **2**
City Hall, **11**
Federal Hall, **7**
Fraunces Tavern, **13**
New York Stock Exchange, **6**
Staten Island Ferry Terminal, **1**
Statue of Liberty, **3**
South Street Seaport, **14**
Trinity Church, **5**
Woolworth Building, **10**
World Financial Center, **9**
World Trade Center, **8**

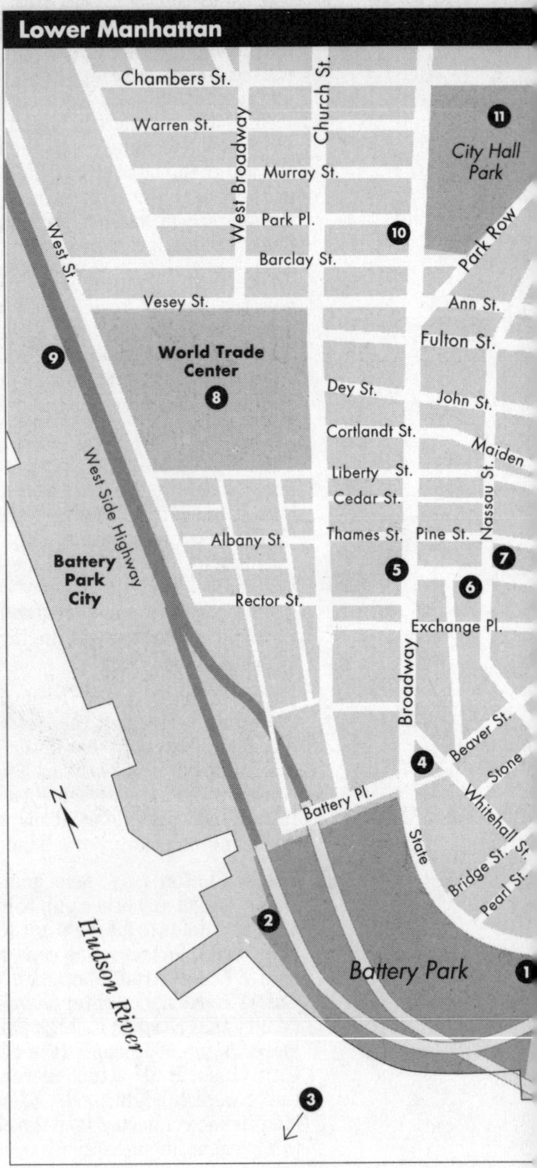

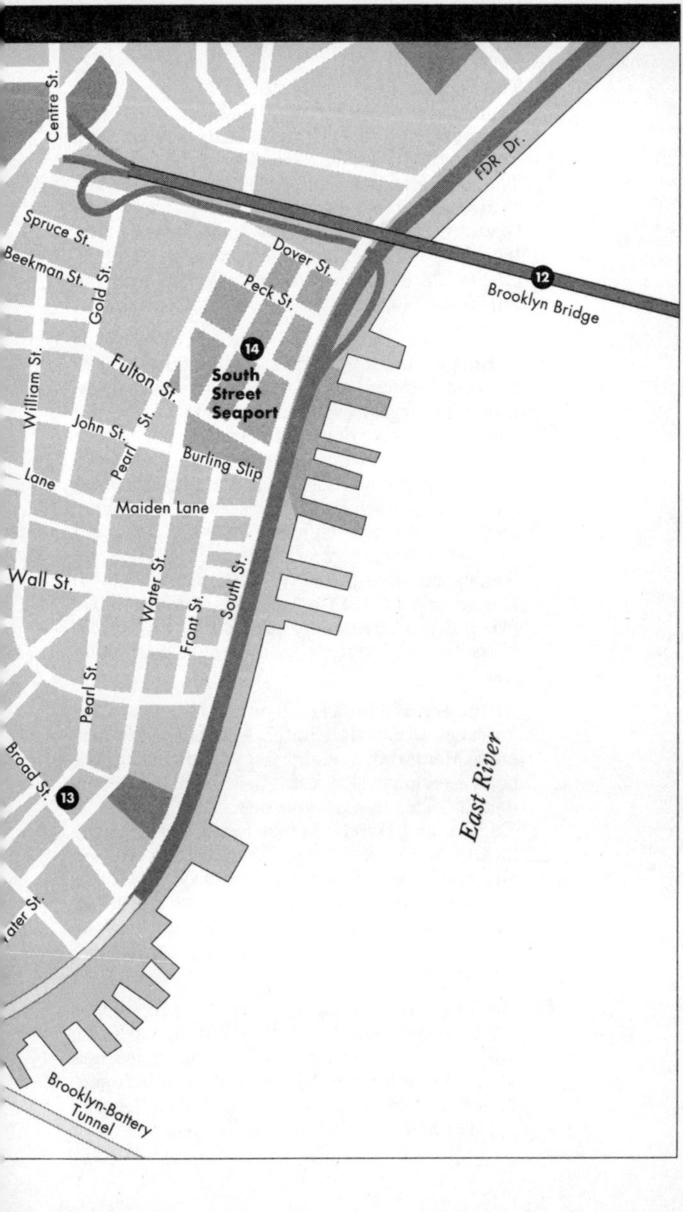
Centre St.
FDR Dr.
Spruce St.
Beekman St.
Gold St.
Dover St.
Peck St.
12
Brooklyn Bridge
14
South
Street
Seaport
William St.
Fulton St.
John St.
Pearl St.
Burling Slip
Lane
Maiden Lane
Wall St.
Water St.
South St.
Front St.
Pearl St.
Broad St.
13
East River
ater St.
Brooklyn-Battery
Tunnel

fort, museum, and ticket office for the Statue of Liberty.

3 The popularity of the **Statue of Liberty** surged following its 100th birthday restoration in 1986. After arriving on Liberty Island, you can take an elevator 10 stories to the top of the pedestal. The strong of heart and limb can climb another 12 stories to the crown. Currently you may have to wait in line for up to three hours for the privilege. *Tel. 212/363–3200. Round-trip fare: $6 adults, $3 children. Daily departures on the half-hour 9–3; extended hours in summer.*

The price of a ticket to the statue includes a visit to **Ellis Island,** which opened in September 1990 to record crowds after a $140 million restoration, the largest-ever U.S. project of its kind (the fund-raising drive was headed by Chrysler Corporation chairman Lee Iacocca). Now a national monument, Ellis Island was once a federal immigration facility that processed 17 million men, women, and children between 1892 and 1954—the ancestors of more than 40% of the Americans living today. *Tel. 212/883–1986. Round-trip fare: $6 adults, $3 children 3–17. Daily departures every 45 minutes 9:30–3:30. Ellis Island Immigration Museum admission free.*

At the end of a broad mall outside the landward entrance to Castle Clinton stands the **Netherlands Memorial,** a quaint flagpole depicting the bead exchange that established Fort Amsterdam in 1626. Inscriptions describe the event in English and Dutch. Across State Street is the facade of the imposing **U.S. Customs House,** adorned by a double row of statuary. The lower statues depict each of the continents; the upper row represents the major trading cities of the world (the woman to the left of the central shield stands for Lisbon).

4 **Bowling Green** is an oval greensward that in 1733 became New York's first public park. On July 9, 1776, a few hours after citizens learned about the signing of the Declaration of Independence, rioters toppled a statue of King George III that had occupied the spot for years.

Broadway begins beside Bowling Green and continues north all the way to Albany. **25 Broadway** used to be headquarters of the Cunard steamship line. The ground floor is now one of the most spectacular post offices you'll ever see, a cathedral of gracious travel with sea gods and mermaids romping across the vaulted ceiling and walls, frescoes depicting great vessels of yore, and richly detailed wall maps of the seven seas. To the left of the vestibule, in a charming niche with an inviting fireplace, is a Philatelic Exhibition Center that displays and purveys commemorative stamps.

George Washington really did sleep at **39 Broadway,** not in the office building now occupying the site, but in the McComb Mansion, which functioned as the second presidential residence between February 23 and August 30, 1790, when it overlooked the Hudson River. The first presidential residence was at 3 Cherry Street, which would now be under the Brooklyn Bridge.

5 **Trinity Church** (Broadway at Wall St.) was established as an Anglican parish in 1697. The present structure (1846) ranked as the city's tallest building for most of the last half of the 19th century. Once completely jet black from decades of pollutants, the exterior sandstone is being restored to its original pink color. Alexander Hamilton is buried beneath a white stone pyramid in Trinity's south-side graveyard; Robert Fulton, the inventor of the steamboat, lies nearby. *Tours daily at 2; free 40-min concerts, Tues. 12:45.*

Arguably the most famous thoroughfare in the world, **Wall Street** was where stock traders used to conduct business along the sidewalks or at tables beneath a sheltering buttonwood tree. Wall
6 Street's principal facility today is the **New York Stock Exchange,** which has its august Corinthian main entrance around the corner on Broad Street. Enter at 20 Broad Street and, after what may be a lengthy wait, take an elevator to the third-floor visitor center. A self-guided tour, informative slide shows, video displays, and guides may help you interpret the chaos that seems to be transpiring down on the trading floor. *Tel. 212/656–5167. Open weekdays*

9:20–3:30. Free tickets available at 20 Broad St. at 9:30.

In building only a two-story investment bank at the corner of Wall and Broad streets, J. P. Morgan was thumbing his nose at Wall Street real estate values. Now **Morgan Guaranty Trust,** the building bears pockmarks near the fourth window on the Wall Street side, created when a bomb in a pushcart exploded in 1920.

A regal statue of George Washington stands at the spot where he was sworn in as the first U.S. president in 1789. The Federal Hall of that day was demolished when the capital moved to Philadelphia. The current **Federal Hall National Memorial** is a stately period structure containing exhibits on New York and Wall Street.

7 Walk through Federal Hall, past the gift shop, and turn right onto Pine Street. You soon reach a plaza around the 65-story **Chase Manhattan Bank Building.** The perimeter of Chase Plaza has become an impromptu flea market for merchandise and fast food, and the interior holds a striking Dubuffet sculpture, *Trees*.

Kitty-corner from the Chase Building, **Louise Nevelson Plaza** occupies the triangle formed by William Street, Liberty Street, and Maiden Lane. The plaza contains benches and four black welded-steel abstract Nevelson sculptures, three middle-size pieces, and one huge 70footer. Sit in the plaza and contemplate the **Federal Reserve Bank** directly across the street. This is a bank that looks like a bank ought to look: gray, solid, imposing, absolutely impregnable—and it had better be, for its vaults reputedly contain a quarter of the world's gold reserves.

Across Maiden Lane from the Fed, take an escalator down to the **Whitney Museum of American Art, Downtown at Federal Plaza,** a free museum that displays 20th-century American art.

8 Continue west on Maiden Lane to the **World Trade Center,** a 16-acre complex that contains New York's two tallest buildings, a hotel, a shopping center, a huge main plaza, and, somewhat incongruously, a farmers' market on Tuesday and Thursday in a parking area along Church Street. The Observation Deck is located

on the 107th floor of 2 World Trade Center, yet the ride up takes only 58 seconds. The view is potentially 55 miles, but signs at the ticket window disclose how far you can see that day and whether the outdoor deck is open. *Admission: $3.50 adults, $1.75 children and senior citizens, children under 6 free. Open daily 9:30 AM–11:30 PM.*

You get the same view with a costly meal at **Windows on the World** atop 1 World Trade Center; prices are somewhat lower for breakfast or for drinks and "grazing" at the **Hors d'Oeuvrerie** (tel. 212/938–1111; jacket required). The TKTS booth (half-price Broadway and Off-Broadway shows) in the mezzanine of 2 World Trade Center is open Monday–Friday 11–5:30, Saturday 11–3:30, earlier than the Times Square location, and has shorter lines.

The rock and soil excavated for the World Trade Center begat **Battery Park City,** a hundred new acres of Manhattan reached by a pedestrian overpass above West Street on the western border of the center. Battery Park City is a complete neighborhood built from scratch. It has office buildings (including the offices of *The Wall Street Journal*), high-rise apartment houses, low-rise old-looking town houses, and a modest selection of shops. Gazing at the Hudson from the placid riverside promenade, you may find it difficult to believe that the New York Stock Exchange lies less than a half-mile away.

9 Battery Park City is also home to the **World Financial Center,** a mammoth granite-and-glass commercial complex designed by architect Cesar Pelli. Inside the four-tower structure is a melange of 30 upscale shops (including Ann Taylor, Barneys New York, Mark Cross, and Godiva Chocolatier), and a palatial public space called the Winter Garden, which has become a popular venue for free performances by top-flight musicians and dancers (tel. 212/945–0505). The room, adorned by a vaulted-glass roof, an immense stairway, and 16 palm trees (carefully transplanted from Borrigo Springs, California), hosts an array of performances through the center's Arts and Events program.

Across Church Street from the World Trade Center stands **St. Paul's Chapel** (Broadway at Fulton St.), the second-oldest structure (1766) in Manhattan and the only surviving example of Colonial architecture. St. Paul's displays George Washington's pew and is open throughout the day for prayer, rest, and meditation.

10 Head north on Broadway to the so-called "Cathedral of Commerce," the ornate **Woolworth Building** (Park Pl. at Broadway). Once the world's tallest building at 792 feet, this agglomeration of architectural styles still houses the Woolworth corporate offices. Sculptures set into arches in the lobby ceiling represent old man Woolworth pinching his pennies and the architect Cass Gilbert contemplating a model of his creation.

Park Row, the street across City Hall Park from the Woolworth Building, was known as "Newspaper Row" from the mid-19th century to the early 20th century, when most of the city's 20 or so daily papers had offices there. Now the city is down to four dailies, and Park Row is an undistinguished commercial strip. In its day, triangular **City Hall Park** hosted hangings, riots, meetings, and demonstrations; much of the time now it accommodates brown-baggers and pigeon feeders.

11 **City Hall,** built between 1803 and 1811, is unexpectedly elegant, sedate, graceful, small-scale, and charming. Its exterior columns reflect the classical influence of Greece and Rome, and the handsome cast-iron cupola is crowned with the statue of lady Justice. The major interior feature is a sweeping marble double staircase. The wood-paneled City Council Chamber in the east wing is small and clubby; the Board of Estimate chamber to the west has Colonial paintings and seating in the church pew manner. Were it not for the metal detectors through which all visitors must pass, you'd think this was a county courthouse in rural Virginia rather than the epicenter of the nation's biggest metropolis.

12 Directly east of City Hall is the **Brooklyn Bridge,** New York's oldest and best known span. When built in 1883 it was the world's longest suspension bridge and, like so many others in

turn, the tallest structure in the city. Now its graceful stone towers no longer seem so awesome. It hasn't been sold to a gullible out-of-towner for years.

Walking across the Brooklyn Bridge is a peak New York experience. The distance is just over a mile, and thousands of commuters make the trip on foot whenever the weather allows. Located in the center of the span, the walkway passes beneath the towers and through the filigree. On the Brooklyn side the span bisects the expansive Watchtower complex operated by the Jehovah's Witnesses. Take the first exit to Brooklyn Heights, a charming neighborhood of brownstones, and head back toward the river to the Promenade for an exciting view of Lower Manhattan.

East Side Directly north of South Ferry stands the **Shrine of St. Elizabeth Ann Seton** (7–8 State St.). The red brick Federal-style town house was built in 1783 as the home of the wealthy Watson family, and Mother Seton dwelled and gave birth to her fifth child in what is now the rectory. Mother Seton went on to found the Sisters of Charity, the first American order of nuns, and in 1975 became the first American-born saint. Masses are held daily.

East of the shrine, State Street becomes Water Street and passes **New York Plaza,** a complex of high-tech office towers linked by an underground concourse. Turn left on Broad Street
13 and you quickly reach **Fraunces Tavern,** a combination restaurant, bar, and museum that occupies a Colonial (brick exterior, cream-colored portico and balcony) tavern built in 1719 and restored in 1907. Best remembered as the site of George Washington's farewell address to his officers celebrating the British evacuation of New York in 1783, Fraunces Tavern contains two fully furnished period rooms and other displays of 18th- and 19th-century American history. *Broad and Pearl Sts., tel. 212/425–1778. Admission: $2.50 adults, $1 students, senior citizens, and children. Restaurant open weekdays. Museum open weekdays 10–4.*

Continuing up Broad Street and turning right on South William Street, you enter an area of curving streets (the routes of old New Amsterdam cowpaths) and low-rise houses that still look much as they did in the 19th century. **Delmonico's,** at the rounded corner of South William and Beaver streets, opened in 1888. The haute cuisine and one of America's first female cashiers made it *the* place to go at the turn of the century. Head east on William Street to **Hanover Square,** a quiet tree-lined plaza that stood on the waterfront when the East River reached Pearl Street. The pirate Captain Kidd lived in the neighborhood, and the brownstone **India House** (1837) used to house the New York Cotton Exchange.

Go one block east to Water Street and turn north
14 to the 11-block **South Street Seaport Historic District.** A reminder of Manhattan's role as a great seaport, this reconstructed 19th-century marketplace, within view of Wall Street's ultramodern skyscrapers, is home to inumerable shops and restaurants, art galleries, old clipper ships, and cruise boats. In spirit linked more closely to other Rouse Corporation waterfront developments in Boston (Quincy Market) and Baltimore (Harborplace) than to the rest of Manhattan, the project still has a lot of appeal.

Schermerhorn Row (2–18 Fulton St.), a series of early 1800s Georgian and Federal-style warehouses, is the Seaport's architectural centerpiece. The ground floors are occupied by shops and bars. The cobblestone street is closed to traffic and, on Friday evening during summer, young professionals from the Financial District stand shoulder-to-shoulder at cocktail hour. The **Fulton Market Building,** which is full of shops and restaurants, re-creates the bustling commercial atmosphere of the old victual markets that were on this site from 1822 on. The 15 restored buildings in **Museum Block,** across Front Street, include Bowne & Co., a reconstructed working 19th-century print shop, and the Museum Shops along twisting Cannon's Walk.

Cross South Street to Pier 16 to view the historic ships: the second-largest sailing ship in existence, *Peking;* the full-rigged *Wavertree;* and the lightship *Ambrose. Admission to ships, gal-*

leries, walking tours, Maritime Crafts Center, films, and other Seaport events: $6 adults, $5 senior citizens, $4 students, $3 children. Open daily 10–5, longer hours in summer.

Pier 16 is the departure point for the 90-minute **Seaport Line Harbor Cruise.** Tel. 212/385–0791. *The fare is $12 adults, $11 senior citizens, $10 students, $6 children.* Notice how two large cargo containers used on modern-day freighters are transformed into a toy shop and a cafe.

Time Out Pier 17 is a multilevel dockside shopping mall. If you're hungry, skip the overpriced seafood joints and head for the fast-food stalls on the third-floor **Promenade Food Court.** Cuisine is nonchain eclectic: Seaport Fries, Pizza on the Pier, Wok & Roll, the Yorkville Packing House for meat, the Salad Bowl for veggies, Bergen's Beer & Wine Garden (10 brews on tap). What's really spectacular is the view of the East River, Brooklyn Bridge, and Brooklyn Heights from the tables in a glass-wall atrium. Seating is on an outdoor deck when weather permits.

As your nose may already have surmised, the blocks along South Street north of the museum complex still house a working fish market. Although the city has tried to relocate the hundreds of fishmongers of the **Fulton Fish Market** in the South Bronx, the area remains a beehive. Get up early if you want to see it: The action begins around midnight and ends by 8 AM.

Continue north to Peck Slip where, on the wall of a building on the north side of the street, you'll see a 90-foot trompe l'oeil mural by Richard Haas showing how that view of the Brooklyn Bridge might have looked 100 years ago. Across the street stands an ornate co-op apartment that used to be **Meyer's Hotel,** where in 1883 Annie Oakley threw a wild rooftop party to celebrate the opening of the Brooklyn Bridge.

Off the Beaten Track

Public Spaces Public spaces go a long way toward making New York a more livable—and visitable—city. Public spaces are created when, in return for receiving a zoning variance, the builders of new office towers agree to design and maintain a portion of the interior space for public use. As such, public spaces perform roles formerly played by public parks and hotel lobbies: They provide clean, safe, physically attractive areas where you can sit, relax, read a newspaper, peruse your guidebook, and watch the world go by. You're welcome to stay as long as you like, and you don't have to spend a dime.

Many of the buildings that have public spaces have turned them into showplaces. And while each indoor park is unique, most of them have features in common. They provide places to sit, such as benches, ledges, and chairs with tables; they have greenery, from potted plants to towering trees; they have fountains or waterfalls to muffle the sounds of the city. Many have snack bars, working telephones, and what can be very difficult to find elsewhere in Manhattan, clean public washrooms.

Buildings with public spaces identify themselves with a logo of a leafy tree over a checkered grid. Public spaces are usually open during the day, and many stay open late into the evening. The following public spaces are listed from Lower Manhattan up.

Continental Insurance Building (180 Maiden La. at Front St.). A modernist atrium just two blocks south of the South Street Seaport Museum. Benches surround copious foliage amid an ultramodern structure that appears to be made of Tinker Toys.

ChemCourt (272 Park Ave. between 47th and 48th Sts.). The Chemical Bank Building provides benches around plantings of exotic shrubs, all helpfully labeled in English and Latin. A glass roof lets the sunshine into the ground floor of the 50-story silver-gray tower.

Olympic Place (645 Fifth Ave., enter on 50th or 51st St.). A splendid space directly opposite St. Patrick's Cathedral and Rockefeller Center, on the ground floor of the brown-tinted Olympic Tower shop, office, and apartment complex. A wall of water drowns out exterior noise. Space includes a Japanese restaurant, a snack bar serving take-out sandwiches and pastries, washrooms, and phones.

Park Avenue Plaza (55 E. 52nd St. between Park and Madison Aves., enter on 52nd or 53rd St.). Conspicuous signs proclaim: "All seating available to public and no purchase of food or beverage required." Nonetheless, most of the tables are covered with tablecloths and table settings for an indoor café, and only a half-dozen tables and chairs at each end of the café are in fact available to the public.

875 Third Avenue (between 52nd and 53rd Sts.). Tables and chairs are on the mezzanine and basement floors. Basement seating is surrounded by an array of fast-food establishments: pizza, bagels, muffins, Chinese buffet, deli, salad bar. The basement also connects with the 53rd Street subway station (E, F lines).

The Market at Citicorp Center (Lexington Ave. at 53rd St.). The distinctive skyscraper whose roof slopes at a 45-degree angle has a thriving three-level atrium lined with restaurants, fast-food stores, and shops. Seating is at tables and chairs and along ledges. The center of the space frequently displays art exhibits or hosts free concerts and movies. Citicorp Center also encompasses the stunning Church of St. Peter's, a Lutheran institution that sold the land the building stands upon and now presents Off-Broadway plays and jazz concerts. Washrooms are on the lower level.

IBM Garden Plaza (56th St. at Madison Ave.). This most spectacular of public spaces has been carved out of the ground floors of the green-granite IBM building. Fully grown bamboo trees rise to the heavens, and seasonal flowers fill the air with fresh scents. The south wall and ceiling are all glass. Seating is available at comfortable chairs and marble tables and on benches beside the plantings. Sandwiches and pastries are sold at a charming round kiosk. The New York Botanical Garden operates a gift shop here, and the free **IBM Gallery of Science and Art** is located off the main lobby. Free concerts Wednesday at 12:30. The atrium connects to Trump Tower, which has phones and washrooms on its lower level.

499 Park Avenue (enter on 59th St.). This is one of the smaller public spaces, and the tinted black windows make it easy to miss. The atrium offers hard benches and a little calmness a block away from Bloomingdale's.

Other Attractions

The Cloisters. Perched atop a wooded hill near Manhattan's northernmost tip, the Cloisters houses part of the Metropolitan Museum of Art's medieval collection in the style of a medieval monastery. Five cloisters connected by colonnaded walks transport you back 700 years. The view of the Hudson and the New Jersey Palisades enhances the experience. The No. 4 "Cloisters-Fort Tryon Park" bus provides a lengthy but scenic ride up there; catch it along Madison Avenue below 110th Street or Broadway above; or take the A subway to the 190th Street station. *Fort Tryon Park, tel. 212/923-3700. Suggested admission: $6 adults, $3 senior citizens and students, children 12 and under free. Open Nov.–Mar., Tues.–Sun. 9:30–4:45; Apr.–Oct., Tues.–Sun. 9:30–5:15.*

General Theological Seminary (Ninth Ave. at 21st St.). This Episcopal institution opened in 1826 on a full city block contributed by Clement "'Twas the night before Christmas" Moore. A secluded Victorian quadrangle enclave of shady trees surrounded by proud ecclesiastical buildings, it is a pleasant refuge from workaday life. A 10-year restoration project is under way.

Roosevelt Island Aerial Tramway (Second Ave. at 60th St.). The high-wire ride to Roosevelt Island, a residential complex in the East River, looks like an oversize Fisher-Price toy. It is a slightly terrifying fun ride that gives you a great view of the city. The one-way fare is $1.40.

Playground at Sixth Avenue and Third Street. Want to see where the NBA hoop stars of tomorrow learn their moves? Check out this patch of Greenwich Village asphalt where city-style basketball is played afternoon and evening in all but the very coldest weather.

Sniffen Court (36th St. between Lexington and Third Aves.). Here is an easy-to-miss cul-de-sac of 19th-century brick stables that were converted into town houses. Equal parts old London and New Orleans, Sniffen Court was for many years the home of the sculptor Malvina Hoffman.

East 90th Street Entrance to Central Park. At this open-air singles hangout for athletes, joggers congregate in the evening to chat, trade training tips, and occasionally run off together.

Paley Park (3 E. 53rd St.). A boon to Midtown's weary, this was the first of New York's "pocket parks" inserted among the high-rise behemoths. A waterfall muffles street noise; a snack bar is open when weather permits.

McGraw-Hill Park (Sixth Ave. between 48th and 49th Sts.). The pocket park behind the McGraw-Hill Building has a stunning walk-through wall of water. Head west on 48th Street to Seventh Avenue, and you'll pass a half-block of stores that sell musical instruments.

Croquet and Lawn Bowling (Central Park, off Central Park West and 69th St.). Clad in spiffy white linen, the croquet players face off on this well-manicured patch of green almost every day of spring and summer.

Conservatory Pond (Central Park, off Fifth Ave. and 74th St.). Radio-controlled model armadas hold miniregattas every Saturday from April through November.

Duane Park (Duane and Hudson Sts.). Surrounded by striking 19th-century masonry buildings, this little triangle in the TriBeCa neighborhood is becoming one of the city's most fashionable addresses. Formerly the center of the dairy industry, horse-drawn egg wagons delivered here until 1954.

Staple Street (west of Hudson St. between Harrison and Duane Sts.). Named for the staple products unloaded here, this narrow alley was where ships in transit through New Amsterdam sold cargo they didn't want to pay duty on. An overhead passage connected sections of the former New York Hospital House of Relief.

Gansevoort Market (around Gansevoort and Greenwich Sts.). Otherwise undistinguished warehouse buildings each morning become the meat market for the city's retailers and restaurants. Racks of carcasses make a fascinating, though not necessarily a very pretty, sight. Action peaks on weekdays 5 AM–9 AM.

Ladies' Mile (Sixth Ave. between 18th and 22nd Sts.). Toward the end of the 19th century, the grand buildings on both sides of the street housed the city's finest department stores, including Simpson-Crawford, O'Neill's, Altman's, and Cammeyers. Trimmed with classical features but now fallen into disrepair, the vast Siegel-Cooper store occupied two-thirds of the block between Fifth and Sixth avenues.

Police Academy Museum (235 E. 20th St., tel. 212/477–9753). Here you can see an emergency procedures display, bizarre weapons, and the latest developments in law-enforcement technology. *235 E. 20th St., tel. 212/477–9753. Admission free. Open weekdays 9–3; large groups by appointment.*

3 Shopping

New York stores are as cosmopolitan and diverse as the city itself. The potential for high profits and world-class visibility motivates consumer-friendly competition at every level. Because merchandise has to attain a sufficiently high standard to please the world's most particular shoppers, costly boutiques and specialty shops abound. Because of the volume of competition in every area, close-out jobbers, off-price dealers, outlet shops, and other sources of discounts abound as well. Whatever you want, you can find it in New York. And if you look a little harder, you can find it selling for less.

In general, major department stores and other shops are open every day and keep late hours on Thursday. Many of the upper-crust shops along Upper Fifth Avenue and the Madison Mile close on Sunday. Stores in such nightlife areas as SoHo and Columbus Avenue are usually open in the evenings. The bargain shops along Orchard Street on the Lower East Side close on Friday afternoon and all day Saturday for the Jewish Sabbath but keep normal hours on Sunday.

Most of the department stores accept their own charge cards and major credit cards, though Lord & Taylor only accepts American Express. Most smaller stores accept major credit cards. Paying by personal check is sometimes permitted but seldom encouraged. Sales tax in New York City is 8¼%.

Shopping Districts

Upper Fifth Avenue. Fifth Avenue from 49th to 58th streets, and 57th Street between Sixth and Third avenues, contains many of the most famous stores in the world, among them Saks Fifth Avenue, Bergdorf Goodman, Henri Bendel, Tiffany & Co., Cartier, and the exclusive shops in Trump Tower.

Herald Square. The area extending from Herald Square (Sixth Ave. and 34th St.) along 34th Street and up Fifth Avenue to 40th Street includes several major stores (Macy's, A&S, Lord & Taylor) and a host of lower-price clothing stores.

Madison Mile. The 20-block span along Madison Avenue between 59th and 79th streets consists of mainly low-rise brownstone buildings housing the exclusive boutiques of American and overseas designers.

SoHo. Along West Broadway between Houston ("How-ston") and Canal streets you'll find galleries, boutiques, avant-garde housewares shops, and shops that defy categorization.

Columbus Avenue. This shopping area between 66th and 86th streets features far-out European and down-home preppie fashions, some antiques and vintage stores, and outlets for adult toys.

Lower East Side. The intersection of Orchard and Delancey streets is a hub for bargains in women's and men's fashions, children's clothing, shoes, accessories, linens. Closed on Saturday; mobbed on Sunday.

South Street Seaport. This historic district's cobbled streets are home to such nationally known retailers as **Ann Taylor, Laura Ashley, Caswell-Massey,** and **Sharper Image,** plus such one-of-a-kind shops as **Hats in the Belfry** and the **Strand** bookstore.

World Financial Center. This elegant new complex in Battery Park City offers a few dozen upscale shops. Most are open on Sundays, when there are often concerts in the glass-domed Wintergarden.

Department Stores

A&S (Sixth Ave. at 33rd St., tel. 212/594–8500). The old Gimbel's, a block south of Macy's, lives again as home to A&S Plaza, whose 120 shops and restaurants on nine floors are anchored by Abraham & Straus, a store well established in the outer boroughs.

Alexander's (Lexington Ave. at 58th St., tel. 212/593–0880). New York's least-expensive full-service department store may surprise you. The men's department features high quality attractive imports; women's sections reward sharp-eyed shoppers.

Shopping Uptown

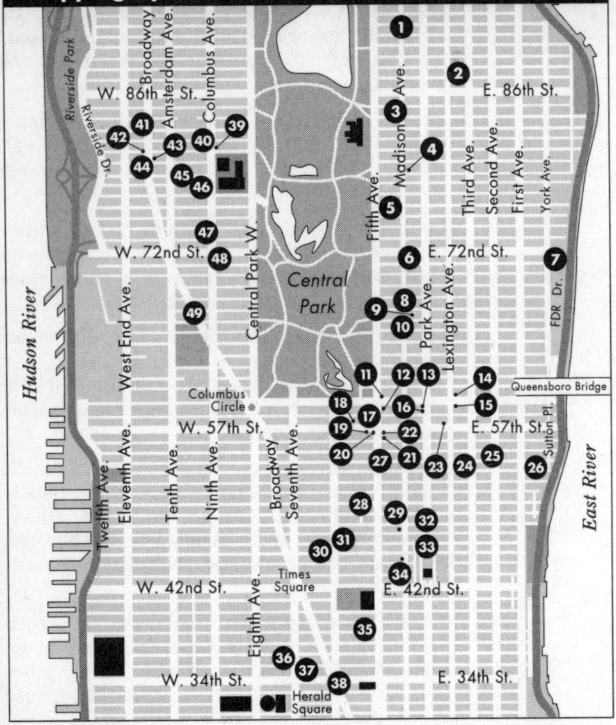

A la Vieille Russie, **11**

Alexander's, **15**

A & S, **38**

American Hurrah, **10**

Anbar, **69**

Barneys, **53**

Ben Farber/Ms., Miss, or Mrs., **36**

Bergdorf Goodman, **17**

Bleeker Bob's Golden Oldies, **59**

Blooming-dale's, **14**

Brooks Brothers, **34**

Canal Jeans, **68**

Charivari, **40, 41, 45, 48**

Christie's, **13**

Citybooks, **70**

Conran's, **24, 42, 57**

Crouch & Fitzgerald, **32**

D.F. Sanders, **5, 64**

Didier Aaron, **9**

Encore, **3**

F.A.O. Schwarz, **12**

Fine & Klein, **66**

Footlight Records, **55**

Forman's, **67**

Fortunoff, **27**

47th Street Photo, **29, 72**

Gotham Book Mart, **31**

Harriet Love, **63**

Henri Bendel, **19**

Israel Sack, **22**

Jazz Record Center, **50**

The Last Wound-Up, **47**

Lord & Taylor, **35**

Shopping Downtown

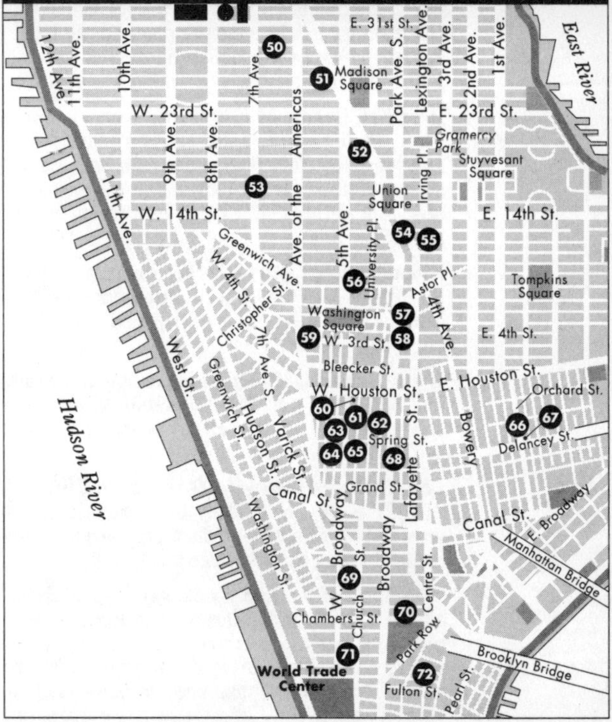

Lubin Galleries, **51**

Macy's, **37**

Manhattan Art & Antiques Center, **25**

Michael's Resale, **4**

Mythology, **46**

New York Bound Book Shop, **28**

Newel Art Galleries, **26**

Patricia Field, **56**

Paul Stuart, **33**

Penny Whistle, **1**, **39**, **65**

Place des Antiquaires, **23**

Polo/Ralph Lauren, **6**

Rizzoli, **18, 60**

Saint Laurie, Ltd., **52**

Saks Fifth Avenue, **29**

Shakespeare & Company, **43**

Sotheby's, **7**

Strand Book Store, **54**

Syms, **71**

T. Anthony, **16**

Tiffany & Co., **21**

Tower Records, **49**, **58**

William Doyle Galleries, **2**

Wolfman-Gold & Good Co., **62**

Ylang Ylang, **8**, **20**

Zabar's, **44**

Zona, **61**

Barneys New York (106 Seventh Ave. at 17th St., tel. 212/929–9000). Famous for its menswear, this retailer has become the place to see what's hot in women's clothing and linens as well. Prices are high, but so are quality and style.

Bergdorf Goodman (754 Fifth Ave., between 57th and 58th Sts., tel. 212/753–7300). A chic and very New York place to shop for women's designer clothes. Head across the street to the new **Men's Store** (745 Fifth Ave.), which opened in August 1990.

Bloomingdale's (at 59th St., Lexington Ave., tel. 212/705–2000). The quintessence of New York style—busy, noisy, crowded, and thoroughly up-to-date.

Henri Bendel (712–716 5th Ave. between 55th and 56th Sts., tel. 212/247–1100). A specialty store made up of many classy boutiques. Prices are not stratospheric.

Lord & Taylor (424 Fifth Ave. at 38th St., tel. 212/391–3344). Not flashy but a relatively uncrowded establishment that emphasizes well-made clothing by American designers.

Macy's (34th St. and Broadway, tel. 212/695–4400). The country's largest retail store occupies 10 stories (nine above ground, one below) and an entire block. Always comprehensive and competitive, Macy's has become quite fashionable as well.

Saks Fifth Avenue (611 Fifth Ave. at 50th St., tel. 212/753–4000). The flagship store of a nationwide chain has an outstanding selection of women's and men's designer outfits.

Flea Markets

Annex Antiques and Flea Market (Sixth Ave. at 25th St.; open weekends 9–5) consists mostly of antiques dealers selling furniture, vintage clothing, books, and jewelry. Admission is charged. The **P.S. 44 Flea Market** (Columbus Ave. at 77th St.; open Sun. 10–6) overflows with clothing, jewelry, books, and collectibles.

Specialty Shops

Antiques

American Hurrah (766 Madison Ave., between 65th and 66th Sts., 3rd floor, tel. 212/535–1930). One of the country's premier dealers in Americana.

Didier Aaron (32 E. 67th St., tel. 212/988–5248). This esteemed gallery specializes in superb 18th- and 19th-century furniture and paintings.

Israel Sack (15 E. 57th St., tel. 212/753–6562). Widely held to be one of the best places to find 18th-century American furniture.

Manhattan Art & Antiques Center (1050 2nd Ave., between 55th and 56th Sts., tel. 212/355–4400). More than 100 dealers stock three floors with antiques from around the world.

Newel Art Galleries (425 E. 53rd St., tel. 212/758–1970). This huge, eclectic gallery is a favorite among local designers.

Place des Antiquaires (125 E. 57th St., tel. 212/758–2900). Two elegant subterranean levels of high-ticket antiques and art dealers.

Auctions

Christie's (502 Park Ave. at 59th St., tel. 212/546–1000). Fine art at suitably fine prices.

Lubin Galleries (30 W. 26th St., tel. 212/924–3777). Reasonably priced furniture and antiques.

Sotheby's (1334 York Ave. at 72nd St., tel. 212/606–7245). Check out the **Arcade** at this famous house, where well-priced also-rans go on the block.

William Doyle Galleries (175 E. 87th St., tel. 212/427–2730). The charismatic William Doyle is at the helm of this major force on the New York auction scene.

Books

Gotham Book Mart (41 W. 47th St., tel. 212/719–4448). A browser's paradise of books on literature and the performing arts.

Rizzoli (31 W. 57th St., tel. 212/759–2424; and two other locations). This elegant shop specializes in the arts.

Shakespeare & Company (2259 Broadway at 81st St., tel. 212/580–7800). The stock represents what's happening in publishing today.

Strand Book Store (828 Broadway at 12th St., tel. 212/473–1452). The biggest of Manhattan's used bookstores.

Cameras, Computers, Electronics **47th Street Photo** (67 W. 47th St., 115 W. 45th St., and 116 Nassau St., tel. 212/398-1410). No hand-holding but great deals.

Food **Zabar's** (2245 Broadway at 80th St., tel. 212/787-2000). From jams, cheeses, spices, and smoked fish to a superb selection of kitchenwares, this store has long been a favorite with New York food lovers.

Fun and Fantasy **Mythology** (370 Columbus Ave., between 77th and 78th Sts., tel. 212/874-0774). Gifts and gadgets with a sense for the fanciful.

Home Decor **Conran's** (Citicorp Center, Third Ave. at 54th St., tel. 212/371-2225; 2248 Broadway at 81st St., tel. 212/873-9250; and 2-8 Astor Pl., tel. 212/505-1515). This is the store that furnishes those chic Manhattan apartments.

D. F. Sanders (386 West Broadway, tel. 212/925-9040; and 952 Madison Ave. at 75th St., tel. 212/879-6161). The slickest of Eurostyle high-tech housewares.

Wolfman-Gold & Good Company (116 Greene St., tel. 212/431-1888). A trendsetter in tableware.

Zona (97 Greene St., tel. 212/925-6750). Handmade work from the Southwest.

Jewelry Every store is a jewelry shop in the **Diamond District** (47th St. between Fifth and Sixth Aves.). Shop around—and be ready to haggle.

A la Vieille Russie (781 Fifth Ave. at 59th St., tel. 212/752-1727). Fabulous antique pieces from Imperial Russia.

Fortunoff (681 Fifth Ave. at 54th St., tel. 212/758-6660). A flashy discount jeweler.

Tiffany & Co. (727 Fifth Ave. at 57th St., tel. 212/755-8000). A venerable institution with prices ranging from out-of-sight to affordable.

Ylang-Ylang (806 Madison Ave. at 67th St., tel. 212/879-7028; 4 W. 57th St., tel. 212/247-3580; and 324 Columbus Ave., tel. 212/496-0319). Outrageous styles of costume jewelry at more or less affordable prices.

Leather and Luggage **Crouch & Fitzgerald** (400 Madison Ave. at 48th St., tel. 212/755-5888). In business since 1839, this is an excellent source for good luggage and handbags.

T. Anthony (480 Park Ave. at 58th St., tel. 212/

750–9797). Exquisitely crafted suitcases and totes.

Discount **Fine & Klein** (119 Orchard St., tel. 212/674–6720). One of Orchard Street's most illustrious discounters.

Menswear **Brooks Brothers** (346 Madison Ave. at 44th St., tel. 212/682–8800). An institution in American menswear, with conservative styles and quality tailoring.

Paul Stuart (Madison Ave. at 45th St., tel. 212/682–0320). At this celebrated, pricy store, the look is traditional without being stodgy.

Saint Laurie, Ltd. (897 Broadway, between 19th and 20th Sts., tel. 212/473–0100). Traditional suits made on the premises at this family-run establishment sell for less than they would uptown.

Discount **Syms** (42 Trinity Pl., tel. 212/797–1199). Designer labels at bargain basement prices. They also have women's clothing.

Records and Tapes **Bleecker Bob's Golden Oldies** (118 W. 3rd St., tel. 212/475–9677). A Greenwich Village spot with all the good old rock.

Footlight Records (113 E. 12th St., tel. 212/533–1572). New York's largest selection of old musical and movie soundtracks.

Jazz Record Center (135 W. 29th St., 12th floor, tel. 212/594–9880). The city's only jazz-record specialist.

Tower Records (692 Broadway at 4th St., tel. 212/505–1500; 1965 Broadway at 66th St., tel. 212/799–2500). A huge selection, with bargain prices, and videotapes galore.

Souvenirs of New York City City souvenirs are widely available, but for something more unusual in tie tacks and T-shirts, try the city-run **Citybooks** (61 Chambers St., tel. 212/669–8245), or stop in at the **New York Bound Bookshop** (50 Rockefeller Plaza, tel. 212/245–8503) for old or rare New York books and prints.

Toys **F.A.O. Schwarz** (767 Fifth Ave. at 58th St., tel. 212/644–9400). A cathedral of childhood delights—with similarly lofty prices.

The Last Wound-Up (290 Columbus Ave., between 73rd and 74th Sts., tel. 212/787–3388; 889 Broadway at 19th St., tel. 212/529–4197). This place offers a mind-boggling selection of wind-up toys.

Penny Whistle Toys (1283 Madison Ave. at 91st St., tel. 212/369–3868; 448 Columbus Ave. at 81st St., tel. 212/873–9090; 132 Spring St., tel. 212/925–2088). Upper East Side, Upper West Side, and SoHo locations for high-tone selection of European and American novelties.

Women's Clothing

Canal Jean (504 Broadway, between Spring and Broome Sts., tel. 212/226–1130). Casual funk draws hip shoppers.

Charivari (2315 Broadway between 83rd and 84th Sts., tel. 212/873–1424). High style, at prices to match, with branches all over the West Side.

Harriet Love (412 W. Broadway, between Prince and Spring Sts., tel. 212/966–2280). This is the doyenne of the city's vintage-clothing scene.

Patricia Field (10 E. 8th St., tel. 212/254–1699). The place to acquire the "downtown" look.

Polo/Ralph Lauren (867 Madison Ave. at 72nd St., tel. 212/606–2100). All the essentials for the Ralph Lauren wardrobe can be found in this grand turn-of-the-century town house.

Discount

Forman's (82 Orchard St., tel. 212/228–2500). An unexpectedly attractive mainstay of the Lower East Side.

Ms., Miss, or Mrs./Ben Farber Inc. (462 Seventh Ave. at 35th St., tel. 212/736–0557). A Garment District establishment with new designer fashions at 30%–60% off.

Discount Shoes

Discounters dot Reade Street between Church and West Broadway, including **Anbar** (93 Reade St., tel. 212/227–0253).

Resale Shops

To pick up top-of-the-line designs at secondhand prices, try **Encore** (1132 Madison Ave. between 84th and 85th Sts., upstairs, tel. 212/879–2850) and **Michael's Resale** (1041 Madison Ave. between 79th and 80th Sts., tel. 212/737–7273).

4 Dining

Name any country, name any city or province in any country, and New York will probably have a *selection* of restaurants specializing in the cuisine of that area.

New York has more than 16,000 restaurants, from world-class temples of the culinary arts to humble cubbyholes serving pizza by the slice or hot dogs New York style, onions and sauerkraut optional. And while not even the most zealous New York food chauvinist would contend that every one of these places is fabulous, competitive pressures do effect a certain level of quality. No New York restaurant is likely to last long if its food doesn't taste good; few restaurants will survive if they don't serve reasonably large portions.

New York restaurants are expensive, yet savvy diners learn how to keep their costs within reason. Since most restaurants post menus in their front windows or lobbies, at least you will have a general idea of what you're getting into. But they don't post drink prices, and these can be high: $3.50 and up for a beer or a glass of wine; $4 and up for mixed drinks (some places charge *considerably* more). To run up your drink bill, many restaurants will ask you to wait in the bar until your table is ready. This occurs even when you have arrived on time and can see plenty of empty tables. While you may have to wait, you don't have to buy a drink.

One way to save money and still experience a top-echelon restaurant is to go there for lunch rather than dinner. It may also be easier to get lunch reservations on short notice.

The slumping economy of the 1990s has worked in favor of the person who wants to eat out in New York. Many restaurants are now offering special fixed-price menus at bargain prices inconceivable a year or two ago. Although reservations are somewhat easier to come by these days, still be sure to make a reservation when you intend to patronize a first-class restaurant. Also, be sure to make a reservation for *any* restaurant on a weekend, especially on Saturday night.

What follows is a selective list of New York restaurants serving a variety of cuisines in all price ranges in neighborhoods throughout Manhattan. As the list can by no means be comprehensive, some of the city's classic restaurants have not been included. In their place, however, you'll find some lesser-known eateries that are frequented by locals. Highly recommended restaurants are indicated by a star ★.

Category	Cost*
Very Expensive	over $60
Expensive	$40–$60
Moderate	$20–$40
Inexpensive	under $20

**per person excluding tax (8¼%), service, and drinks*

The following credit card abbreviations are used: AE, American Express; DC, Diners Club; MC, Mastercard; V, Visa.

American/Continental

Very Expensive ★

Four Seasons. Menus and decor shift with the seasons in this class act. The bright and spacious Pool Room has a marble pool, changing floral displays, paintings by Picasso, Miró, and Rauschenberg. It's the rosewood Grill Room, however, where movers and shakers rendezvous for Power Lunches. Both settings have wide open spaces, impeccable service—and very high prices. An imaginative and unpredictable menu puts an Oriental spin on traditional American and French cuisine. Roast duck and pepper steak are reliable choices. The Spa Cuisine menu appeals to weight-watchers; lower-priced pre- and post-theater menus (5–6:15 and 10–11:15) at $41.50 please wallet-watchers. *The Seagram Building, 99 E. 52nd St., tel. 212/754-9494. Reservations required, in advance for weekends. Jacket required. AE, DC, MC, V. Closed Sat. lunch and Sun.*

Expensive

Arizona 206. The ambience of the American Southwest is captured a block away from Bloomingdale's: stark white plaster walls, wood-burning fireplace, raw timber trimming,

Dining Uptown

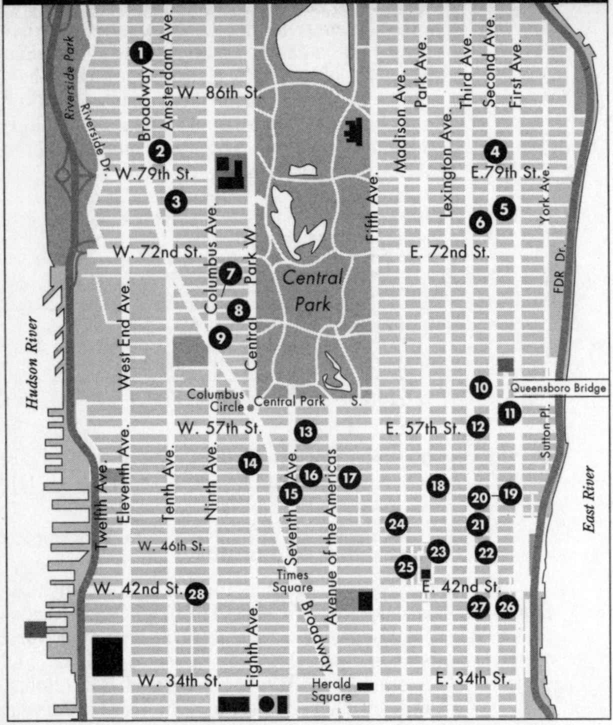

Alcala, **3**
Amsterdam's Bar and Rotisserie, **2**
Arizona 206, **10**
Bangkok Cuisine, **14**
Café des Artistes, **8**
Chez Josephine, **28**
China Grill, **17**
Dawat, **12**
Dock's, **1, 27**
Extra! Extra!, **26**
Four Seasons, **18**
The Ginger Man, **9**
Grand Central Oyster Bar, **25**
Hatsuhana, **23, 24**
J.G. Melon, **6**
Le Bernardin, **15**
Lutèce, **20**
Pig Heaven, **4**
Remi, **16**
Rosa Mexicana, **11**
Russian Tea Room, **13**
Smith & Wollensky, **21**
Sparks Steak House, **22**
Vašata, **5**
Vince & Eddie's, **7**
Zarela, **19**

Dining Downtown

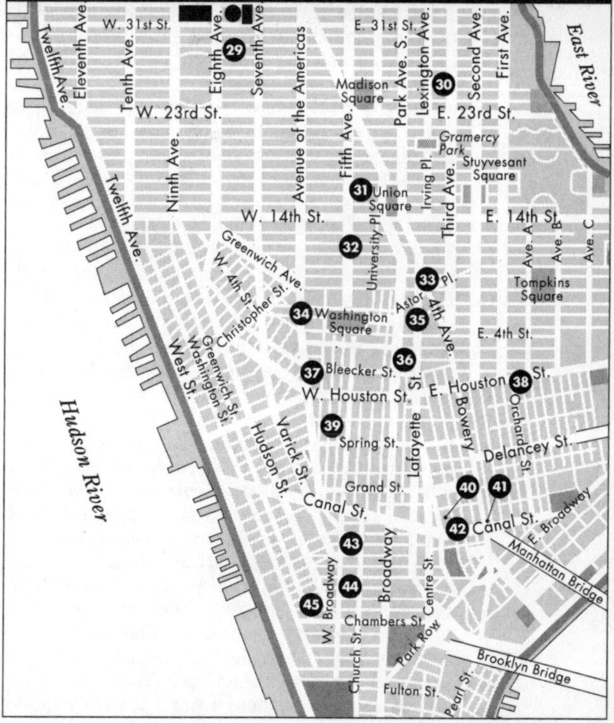

Acme Bar and Grill, **36**
The Ballroom, **29**
Coach House, **34**
La Colombe D'Or, **30**
Gotham Bar & Grill, **32**
Indochine, **35**
Il Cortile, **40**
Katz's Delicatessen, **38**
Montrachet, **43**
Odeon, **44**
Omen, **39**
Silver Palace, **41**
Siracusa Gourmet Café, **33**
Tommy Tang's, **45**
Union Square Cafe, **31**
Villa Mosconi, **37**
Wong Kee, **42**

and piped-in Willie Nelson records. The New American-Southwestern cuisine stresses chili peppers, and the brief menu (by chef Beth Valley) offers nothing ordinary, only the likes of smoked-sturgeon quesadilla; grilled salmon steak with *poblano* corn custard; and black-bean cakes with dandelion greens and Cajun crawfish. Desserts are just as unusual, and the service staff is downright perky. *206 E. 60th St., tel. 212/838–0440. Reservations advised. Dress: casual. AE, DC, MC, V. No lunch Sun.*

The Coach House. Opened in the late 1940s, this genteel West Village dining spot serving traditional American cuisine seems lost in another long-ago, slower paced time period, with its wood-shuttered windows, charming equestrian-themed oil paintings, rose-colored tablecloths, and copper pots. Red banquettes along brick and wood-paneled walls and fresh flowers in ceramic jugs around the room add to the homey, old-fashioned atmosphere. Begin your meal with the mouth-watering cornsticks, cold eggplant Provençale, deviled crab cake, or black bean soup madeira. Meat and fish entrées are well prepared, especially roast ribs of beef, rack of spring lamb, and fish poached in bouillon; vegetables and potatoes, however, receive a more lackluster presentation. The hearty desserts include an excellent apple tart with fresh whipped cream and the Coach House chocolate ice-cream cake. Although you'll probably spend a pleasant evening here, you may find this place disappointing, especially if you're seeking exceptional or more exciting fare. *110 Waverly Pl. (near Ave. of the Americas), tel. 212/777–0303. Reservations required weekends. Jacket advised. AE, DC, MC, V. Closed Mon.*

★ **Gotham Bar and Grill.** A place with a name like Gotham better be huge, crowded, the quintessence of sophistication—and that's what this is. Owned by a former New York City commissioner, the Gotham Bar and Grill has a postmodern decor with tall columns, high ceilings decked with parachute shades, a pink-marble bar, and a striking pink-green-black color scheme. The menu is eclectic and surprising: Try veal carpaccio or roasted quail salad. *12 E. 12th St., tel. 212/620–4020. Reservations advised. Dress: casual. AE, DC, MC, V. No lunch weekends.*

Moderate

Amsterdam's Bar & Rotisserie. The name tells most of the story: It's basically a bar on the Upper West Side's Amsterdam Avenue where most of the food is prepared on an open rotisserie. Low prices for roasted poultry (chicken and duck are tops) and beef dishes accompanied by a vegetable and an ambitious house salad elicit standing-room crowds late into the night. Fish dishes are also good and homemade ketchup graces every table. *428 Amsterdam Ave. between 80th and 81st Sts., tel. 212/874–1377. No reservations. Dress: casual. AE, DC, MC, V.*

The Ginger Man. The Ginger Man could hold its own as a hearty, desirable West Side stop even if it weren't a mere stone's throw from Lincoln Center. Simple, satisfying fare plus warm, dignified service guarantee this cozy bar and its two dining areas as a fine meeting place for conversation and people-watching. Preface your dinner of roast rack of lamb or sautéed duck breast with either the Caesar salad or the chilled gazpacho, but skip the desserts. At 8 PM, the theater crowd clears and an inexpensive supper menu becomes available featuring burgers, sandwiches, and a selection of low-cholesterol omelettes. *51 W. 64th St. (off Broadway), tel. 212/399–2358. Reservations advised for 5–8 PM. Dress: casual. AE, DC, MC, V.*

Odeon. A converted Art Deco cafeteria in the TriBeCa neighborhood south of SoHo and north of the Financial District, it's a popular hangout with the SoHo art set. The menu mingles French brasserie-style dishes with purely American fare. Steak and *frites* or poached lotte in fennel-saffron broth are good choices. *145 West Broadway at Thomas St., tel. 212/233–0507. Reservations advised. Dress: casual. AE, DC, MC, V. No lunch Sat.*

★ **Union Square Café.** A young, monied crowd frequents this site, mere feet from the greenery of renovated Union Square. Light-wood floors and cream-colored walls splashed with Chagall-esque murals lend a bit of airiness to the awkward layout of the three dining areas. Executive chef Michael Romano uses rustic touches in such appetizers as fried calamari in anchovy mayonnaise and entrées like grilled marinated filet mignon of tuna and lemon-pepper duck. Some diners choose to make a meal from the extensive selection of vegetables, which includes mashed turnips with fried shallot crisps and hot garlic potato chips. Recommended desserts include the warm banana tart or chocolate-stuffed soufflé cupcake with espresso custard sauce. *21 E. 16th St., tel. 212/243–4020. Reservations advised. Jacket advised. AE, DC, MC, V. Closed Sun.*

Inexpensive ★ **J.G. Melon.** This is the ideal place for a relaxing and casual meal. A real "neighborhood" pub, with locations on both the East and West sides, Melon's consistently makes people feel at home. Decorated with countless paintings, and prints of (what else?) melons, the bar/restaurant is a good spot in which to meet people or have a laid-back American meal. The burgers and club sandwiches are always a good choice, accompanied by crispy cottage fries. *1291 3rd Ave. at 74th St., tel. 212/744–0585; 340 Amsterdam Ave., tel. 212/877–2220. No reservations. Dress: casual. No credit cards.*

Vince & Eddie's. In a neighborhood sorely lacking in inexpensive eating spots, this recent arrival to the Lincoln Center area offers hearty American fare at reasonable prices. Low, beamed ceilings, sturdy oak furniture, and rough whitewashed walls lend Vince & Eddie's a country-inn flavor, though the intimate atmosphere can turn intrusive when the restaurant is busy. Service is friendly but brusque; best to dine after 8 PM, when you can savor your meal at leisure. Relax in the bar, nestled in a wing chair by the fireplace, before joining the largely preppy crowd inside where you can enjoy such dishes as baked mussels in extra-virgin olive oil, a moist red snapper with pecans, and succulent duck with bourbon sauce. You'll want to try at least one of the imaginative vegetables side dishes—the mashed turnips with shallot crisps, for example—but be forewarned: These are à la carte and can inflate your bill. Homemade sorbet and ice cream and a light, creamy cheesecake make refreshing finales. The wine selections provide good value but are decidedly lackluster. In warm weather, you can dine in the garden patio beneath a 150-year-old tree. *70 W. 68th St. (between Central Park W and Colum-*

bus Ave.), tel. 212/721–0068. Reservations required. Dress: casual. AE, DC, MC, V.

Cajun

Inexpensive **Acme Bar and Grill.** From the outside, you might mistake this restaurant for a warehouse and never discover the narrow, noisy dining area opening up to a bar behind its large metal doors. This is not the place for delicate dining—from its mismatched chairs with ripped upholstery and wood tables bearing vintage hot-sauce ads to its ample portions of down-home southern cooking, there's nothing pretentious about a meal here. The kitchen serves up plenty of seafood, including plump fried oysters and farm-raised catfish, but it also produces delicious corn fritters, a wonderful Cajun peanut soup, Cajun chicken, and an incredibly rich chocolate mud pie as part of its repertoire. The dishes arriving at your table are not very spicy, but the bottles of hot sauces lining the exposed-brick walls should serve to satisfy the most avid heat enthusiast. *9 Great Jones St. (near Broadway), tel. 212/420–1934. No reservations. Dress: casual. No credit cards.*

Chinese

Note: Chinese food is a staple of the New York diet. Most restaurants serve interchangeable menus that combine dishes from various areas of China and use a star or red lettering to indicate spicy dishes. With few exceptions the food is good and truly inexpensive (about $10 per person). Chinese restaurants typically offer low-priced lunch specials—soup, egg roll, main dish, tea—for between $4.50 and $6. Restaurants listed here offer something more than the typical neighborhood Chinese place. You can't go wrong, either, with any busy restaurant in Chinatown—the area bordered by Canal Street on the north, and the Bowery on the east.

Moderate **Pig Heaven.** This popular Upper East Side restaurant is gimmicky to the max. A cutout pig greets you with the menu; wallboards are painted a shocking pig pink; tea is served in pigsnout mugs. Yet the food is serious. Pork dominates the menu, with about 20 nightly specials available. Try Cantonese-style suckling pig or minced pork sautéed with corn, peppers, and pine nuts. Patience may be called for when big crowds slow up the mostly non-Oriental service staff. *1540 Second Ave. at 80th St., tel. 212/744–4333. Reservations advised on weekends. Dress: casual. AE, DC, MC, V.*

Inexpensive **Silver Palace.** The draw here on weekends is dim sum, a parade of dishes wheeled around the banquet-size second-floor dining room on carts that stop at each table for diner's to sample from at random. The steamed dumplings contain tasty fillings (the shrimp is particularly good), and the fried dumplings are light and delicately flavored. From the exotic (curried squid) to the familiar (barbecued beef on a stick), there's something here to please everybody. Portions are small, but you'll fill up fast. The tables are large, and no chair goes unused for long, so you'll probably join a meal that's already in progress. *52 Bowery, tel. 212/964–1204. Reservations not accepted for dim sum. Dress: casual. AE, DC, MC, V (no cards accepted before 6 PM). Dim sum served weekends 8–4 only.*

Wong Kee Restaurant. Diners gather behind the columned, brushed metal facade for the renowned barbecued pork, or the spiced beef chow fun (wide rice noodles), or maybe the sweet and pungent chicken (a refinement of sweet-and-sour), all highlights on this menu. Wong Kee's hallmark is the reliability of its low-priced, high-quality Cantonese fare, made with fresh ingredients and served in ample portions. Service is swift, but expect to wait for a table on weekends. Take-out is also available, and nearly irresistible. *113 Mott St. (north of Canal St.), tel. 212/226–9018. Reservations advised on weekends. Dress: casual. BYOB. No credit cards.*

Czechoslovak

Moderate **Vašata.** A cozy Czech restaurant that has been serving hearty food since 1952. Vašata is a survivor in a neighborhood once full of East European places. Except for a few touches of American '50s decor, this place has the look of a homey Old World wine cellar—lanterns and colorful ceramic dishes decorate pale-yellow brick walls. It's still very popular with émigrés, who come for the goulash, schnitzel, roast duck, dumplings, and genuine Pilsner Urquell beer. You'll feel pleasantly stuffed by the end of the meal, but whatever you do, don't leave without sampling the *palačinky*, delicate dessert crepes with fruit or chocolate filling, doused in orange liqueur and flambéed at the table. *339 E. 75th St. (near 1st Ave.), tel. 212/988–7166. Reservations advised. Dress: casual. AE, MC, V. No lunch except Sun. Closed Mon.*

Deli

Inexpensive **Katz's Delicatessen.** This Kosher-style New York delicatessen in the heart of the Lower East Side can get a bit chaotic at times. There is a method to the madness, however: grab a ticket when you enter, give it to the counterman as you shout your order, and hold on to it to pay the bill when you leave. You might recognize your surroundings—walls and ceilings hung with war memorabilia and hanging salamis—from the film *When Harry Met Sally*. The noise level can be a bit much, but so are the portions, so come hungry. Classics from knishes, pastrami, and brisket to the neighborhood's famous pickles—are all here, and if you like corned beef, it's a must. *205 E. Houston St. (near Orchard St.), tel. 212/254–2246. No reservations. Dress: casual. AE.*

French

Very Expensive ★ **Lutèce.** There isn't anyone who doesn't adore Lutèce, a temple of classic French gastronomy for over 25 years. The intimate and understated midtown town house has seating around an enclosed garden or in two more formal upstairs chambers. The regular menu is varied and specials change daily; grilled trout and pheasant are always fine choices. The impeccable service is invariably attentive and helpful, to first-time and hundredth-time diners alike. *249 E. 50th St., tel. 212/752–2225. Reservations required 2 weeks or more in advance. Jacket and tie required. AE, DC, MC, V. No lunch Mon. and Sat.; closed Sun. and Aug.*

Expensive
★ **Café des Artistes.** A romantic and extremely popular Lincoln Center area institution. Murals of nudes cavorting in a sylvan glade and sparkling mirrors transport you far from the madding Manhattan crowd. Food is country French and includes *confit* of duck with *flageolet* beans and herb-crusted tuna steak—both are recommended specialties. The place crowds up with West Side locals and out-of-towners. *1 W. 67th St. at Central Park West, tel. 212/877–3500. Reservations required. Jacket required at dinner. AE, DC, MC, V.*

★ **Montrachet.** A neighborhood French restaurant—the neighborhood is TriBeCa—that evokes the flavor of backstreet Paris. Inside, the ambience is spare but attractive—wood tables with white cloths, dusty-rose banquettes, carpeting throughout—and the mood is chummy. The menu favors fresh full-flavored Provençale-style concoctions of seafood (black sea bass, lobster, red snapper) and fowl (pheasant with orzo and olives, duck with ginger). *239 West Broadway (near White St.), tel. 212/219–2777. Reservations advised. Dress: casual. AE. Closed Sun. Lunch Fri. only.*

Moderate
★ **Chez Josephine.** The reincarnation of a former massage parlor on West 42nd Street into a 1920s era bistro is Jean-Claude Baker's tribute to his second mother, Josephine Baker. Mr. Baker is in the process of writing a biography of Josephine, so his knowledge of the age is extensive. After installing the long, narrow space with what he considers to be the most important element—a piano and singer—he has added red-velvet drapes, ceiling fans, and murals and posters of Ms. Baker. Though he says "I'm no soup seller," Mr. Baker does a creditable job in the food department also. Entrées such as leg of lamb marinated in juniper berries on a bed of *pomme purée* and carrots, and lobster cassoulet with seafood sausage not to mention the thick accent of the waitress, give the impression of dining in a somewhat funky Montmarte bistro. And the West 42nd Street location appeals to the pre- and post-theater crowd. *414 W. 42nd St. (west of Ninth Ave.), tel. 212/594–1925. Reservations advised. Dress: casual. AE, MC, V. Closed Sun. and lunchtime.*

★ **La Colombe D'Or.** Pots of geraniums by the front door, lace curtains at the windows, and interior walls of rough white plaster and exposed brick set a cozy bistro atmosphere, carried out by friendly, unfawning service. The food, however, goes well beyond standard bistro fare, with creative combinations such as seared sea scallops with broccoli rabe and brazed endive, grilled salmon with chanterelle mushrooms and lettuce, or a surprisingly succulent calves' liver with carrots and grilled sweet onions. Each plate is arranged as beautifully as a still life. The wine list is long, decidedly French, and well priced. *134 E. 26th St. (near Lexington Ave.), tel. 212/689–0666. Reservations advised. Dress: casual. AE, DC, MC, V. Closed Sat. lunch and Sun.*

Indian

Moderate ★ **Dawat.** A sophisticated note is struck at once by softly lit, simple decor, colored in peach and aqua and accented by gleaming copper serving dishes. Classic Indian food, following the recipes of actress-author Madhur Jaffrey, carries out the promise with savory and often spicy dishes, including several vegetarian specialties and robust breads. Try the tandoori mixed grill, baked in its clay oven, the *rogan josh* (baby goat in cardamom sauce), or the *farasvi bhaji* (green beans in coconut). Lunch specials are an excellent value. *210 E. 58th St. (near 3rd Ave.), tel. 212/355–7555. Reservations advised. Dress: casual. AE, DC, MC, V.*

Italian

Moderate ★ **Il Cortile.** This classy establishment is one of the brightest spots in the sea of restaurants for which Little Italy is famous. Dark colors and exposed brick set a warm, intimate tone in the front dining room (try for a table by the window), while the back rooms of the restaurant are brightened by a skylight and an abundance of greenery. Dishes are well prepared and presented—try the simple *scaloppine di vitello al cognac* (tender slices of veal smothered in mushrooms and a cognac gravy) or any of the fresh seafood dishes. Desserts here do not live up to the standard set by the earlier courses, and diners would do better to venture into one of the neighborhood's numerous pastry shops for dessert and espresso. *125 Mulberry St. (near Hester St.), tel. 212/226–6060. Reservations advised. Dress: casual. AE, DC, MC, V.*

★ **Remi.** This chic and sophisticated Italian restaurant offers consistently wonderful food, a festive atmosphere, and stunning interior design. A huge mural of the Grand Canal in Venice is a dramatic backdrop for the elegant blue and white upholstery, the Venetian glass chandeliers, the wood floor inlaid with stripes of Brazilian cherry and maple, and the well-dressed waiters; there isn't a detail in the place (including the space itself) that isn't special. Happily, the food is no exception. The creative menu featuring Northern Italian cuisine is so enticing, you'll agonize over what to choose. Especially delicious is the daily risotto special (whatever it is, it's always fabulous), *fegato alla Veneziana* (calf's liver with carmelized onions), served with fresh polenta, and *galetto al forno* (grilled free-range Cornish hen). As if all this weren't enough, the service is impeccable. *145 W. 53rd St. (near 7th Ave.), tel. 212/581–4242. Reservations advised. Dress: jacket advised. AE, DC, MC, V. Closed for lunch on weekends.*

Siracusa Gourmet Café. A rather eclectic decor—clean-lined Art Deco combined with Italian folk art—sets the tone for this charming Italian eatery, where country-style Sicilian recipes are geared toward sophisticated palates. Some of the excellent pastas are *pasticciotto* (pasta stuffed with zucchini, ricotta, mushrooms, and pignoli nuts) and tagliarini *campagna* with sausage and tomato. The desserts are what really stand out here, however; if you don't feel like coming for a meal, stop by the *gelateria* next door and enjoy such flavors as ricotta, cappuccino, or chocolate—all made on the premises and wonderfully creamy. *65 4th Ave. (near 10th St.), tel. 212/254–1940. Reservations advised. Dress: casual. AE. Closed Sat. lunch and Sun.*

Villa Mosconi. In the heart of Greenwich Village, this authentic trattoria spins you back to a simpler time. Genial chef and proprietor Pietro Mosconi takes special care of the diners who nightly crowd the cozy dining room, decorated with Old World paintings. The ingredients are as fresh as can be. Seafood comes straight from the stalls of the Fulton fish market and all pastas are made on the premises. The menu includes dishes such as tortellini with four cheeses, veal bolognese with prosciutto and cheese in wine sauce, and shrimp scampi alla Mosconi. *69 MacDougal St. (between Houston and Bleecker Sts.), tel. 212/673–0390. Reservations advised. Dress: casual. AE, DC, MC, V. Closed Sun.*

Japanese

Moderate ★ **Hatsuhana.** The authenticity of Hatsuhana's two bright and cheerful Midtown locations is verified by conspicuous contingents of visiting Japanese businessmen. They come for ultra-fresh sushi and sashimi, which are best enjoyed close up at the sushi bar. Other recommended items include bite-size Japanese fried crabs, ungreasy Japanese fried chicken, and any of the grilled fish teriyaki. *17 E. 48th St., tel. 212/355–3345; 237 Park Ave. at 46th St., tel. 212/661–3400. Reservations required. Jacket and tie advised. AE, MC, V. Closed weekends.*

Omen. Old brick, hardwood floors, timber ceilings, and Oriental lanterns give this SoHo ex-store the relaxing ambience of a Japanese country inn. *Omen* is the name of an opening dish almost everybody orders. It's a dark hot broth served with half-cooked exotic vegetables, sesame seeds, and noodles that you add to the soup. Other favorites include a boned chicken dish called *sansho*, scallops and spinach with sesame cream, and avocado with shrimp in miso sauce. *113 Thompson St. between Spring and Prince Sts., tel. 212/925–8923. Reservations advised. Dress: casual. Closed lunch and Mon. AE, DC.*

Mexican

Expensive **Zarela.** Refined Mexican cuisine is served at this Upper East Side spot. The menu features lightly seasoned *fajitas* (skirt steak), *salpicon* (red snapper), and tuna with mole sauce. Diners occupy heavy wooden chairs and brightly cushioned benches which are positioned along a white brick wall. Piñatas, crepe paper streamers, and lively Mexican music add a festive touch. *953 Second Ave. at 51st St., tel. 212/644–*

6740. Reservations advised. Dress: casual. AE, DC. Closed lunch weekends.

Moderate **Rosa Mexicano.** This is a crowded midtown hangout for young professionals. Serious dining takes place amid subdued pink stucco walls and lush horticulture. Two standard Mexican items are exceptional here: chunky *guacamole* prepared at your table and margaritas blended with pomegranate. Grilled versions of shell steak, chicken, and snapper; pork *carnitas;* and skinned breast of duck are other house specialties. *1063 First Ave. at 58th St., tel. 212/753–7407. Reservations advised. Dress: casual. AE, DC, MC, V.*

Mixed Menu

Moderate **China Grill.** This stark restaurant, located in the CBS building, has endured in atmosphere and quality since its opening in 1987. The sleek room is orange and slate gray with huge kite-like lights on the 40-foot ceiling, and although spacious, it tends to get noisy quickly. Described as being French-American with oriental accents, the menu is an assortment of grilled dishes, with an emphasis on fish. Start the meal with the Peking duck salad, which is minced to perfection and served in a tangerine and orange sauce. The entrées are served on oversized plates with portions to match. The grilled dry aged Szechuan beef with shredded potatoes and the stir-fried sea scallops with Chinese noodles make a nice combination. On the side, and not to be missed is the crispy spinach, which literally melts in your mouth. To top off the meal indulge in chocolate-and-amaretto parfait. *52 W. 53rd St. (off 6th Ave.), tel. 212/333–7788. Reservations advised. Jacket advised. AE, DC, MC, V. Closed Sun.*

Inexpensive **Extra! Extra!** Black and white walls peppered with giant newsprint seem appropriate for this fun spot, located in the Daily News building. Life-size comic strip cutouts look on as diners feast on pasta salads, sandwiches, and pizzas. The eclectic menu includes such appetizers as Louisiana fresh-grilled alligator sausage and fresh-fried *calamari,* as well as popular entrées such as crab cakes and chicken *fajitas.* It's an especially lively locale for lunch. *767 2nd Ave. at 41st St., tel. 212/490–2900. Reservations advised. Dress: casual. AE, DC, MC, V. Closed Sat. and Sun.*

Russian

Expensive ★ **Russian Tea Room.** Russian food is probably the last reason to eat here. Located beside Carnegie Hall, the Russian Tea Room is a major New York scene loaded with media people, their agents, and kindred would-be deal cutters. (Dustin Hoffman lunched here with his agent in *Tootsie.*) It's also filled with local commoners and out-of-towners, some of whom get exiled to the celebrityless second-floor—"Siberia." Best menu choices are hot or cold borscht, *karsky shashlik* (lamb with kidneys), and a selection of red and black caviars rolled into tender *blini* (pancakes). *150 W. 57th St., tel. 212/265–0947. Reservations advised. Jacket required at dinner. AE, DC, MC, V.*

Seafood

Very Expensive ★ **Le Bernardin.** The New York branch of an illustrious Paris seafood establishment occupies the ground floor of the midtown Equitable Assurance Tower; the elegant corporate decor was reportedly inspired by the Equitable boardroom. The all-seafood menu teems with rare treasures. For starters, try black bass flecked with coriander or sea urchins baked in their shell. Go on to *rouelle* of salmon sautéed with fennel julienne or any of the fresh, artfully arranged fillets. *155 W. 51st St., tel. 212/489–1515. Reservations required. Jacket and tie required. AE, DC, MC, V. Closed Sun.*

Expensive ★ **Grand Central Oyster Bar & Restaurant.** Down in the catacombs beneath Grand Central Terminal, the Oyster Bar has a reputation for serving ultrafresh seafood. The vast main room has a vaulted tile ceiling, and lots of noise and tumult. Solos may prefer to sit at the wide white counter. By contrast, the wood-paneled Saloon feels downright clubby. More than a dozen varieties of oysters may be on hand. Pan-roasted shellfish, a kind of stew, is a house specialty. Broiled fillets change with the daily catch. *Lower level*

Grand Central Terminal, 42nd St. at Vanderbilt Ave., tel. 212/490–6650. Reservations advised, required for lunch. Dress: casual. AE, DC, MC, V. Closed Sat. and Sun.

Moderate **Dock's.** The fresh fish in this natty Upper West Side bistro serves as a delicious reminder that New York is, after all, a seaport. Classy and unpretentious, Docks has earned a loyal clientele at both this and its east side location (633 Third Ave. at 40th St.). The crab cakes here are the best in town, and all frying is done with a light touch, with seasonings that enhance—not overpower—the fish's flavor. Whether grilled or broiled, the salmon and tuna dishes are excellent, and the shellfish is consistently pleasing. There is an extensive selection of beers, and the wine list is tailored to complement seafood. Try to leave room for the chocolate mud cake or the Key lime pie. *2427 Broadway, at 90th St., tel. 212/724–5588; 633 Third Ave. at 40th St., tel. 212/986–8080. Reservations advised. Dress: casual. AE, DC, MC, V.*

Spanish

Moderate **Alcala.** Visit this Spanish restaurant and tapas bar for the tranquil atmosphere and the varied menu. The large, exposed brick-walled room gives diners an opportunity to relax over a wide variety of seafood, fish, chicken, and beef dishes. Appetizers such as fried calamari and cream of cauliflower soup far surpass the entrées. Try the homemade ice cream and sherbets for dessert. *349 Amsterdam Ave. (near 76th St.), tel. 212/769–9600. Reservations advised. Dress: casual. AE, DC, MC, V. Dinner only.*

The Ballroom. Located in Chelsea a few blocks from Penn Station, this is the place to sample tapas, Spanish appetizers that quickly accumulate into a full meal. Some like their tapas hot—grilled eggplant, stuffed squid, baked fennel, sauteed shiitake mushrooms, baby lamb chops. Others prefer them cold—octopus in oil, bay scallops, *chorizos* (sausage) with peppers, chicken with tomato. The spacious, palmy setting focuses on a huge mural of local painters and art dealers. A popular cabaret theater occupies a separate room. *253 W. 28th St., tel. 212/*

244–3005. Reservations advised. Dress: casual. AE, DC, MC, V. Closed Mon.

Steaks

Expensive

★ **Smith & Wollensky.** This midtown steak house opened only 14 years ago, but plank floors, bentwood chairs, and walls decked with classic sporting prints make it look like it's been here forever. Steak is the forte of this establishment, big blackened sirloins and filets mignon with a pepper sauce. Huge lobsters, veal chops, and terrific onion rings round out the menu. *201 E. 49th St. at Third Ave., tel. 212/753–1530. Reservations advised. Jacket advised. AE, DC, MC, V.*

★ **Sparks Steak House.** Steaks and male camaraderie are the specialties of this midtown restaurant. The tender prime sirloin is the most popular selection. Filets are unusually juicy and flavorful; lobsters cruise the three- to five-pound range. Although most of the ex-athlete-size customers seem to go for beer or whiskey, Sparks boasts an award-winning wine list. *210 E. 46th St., tel. 212/687–4855. Reservations required. Jacket and tie advised. AE, DC, MC, V. Closed Sun.*

Thai

Moderate

Tommy Tang. This exuberant TriBeCa Thai restaurant, set in a bright, high-ceilinged long room with Art Deco-ish decor of turquoise and beige, has mellowed a bit since it opened in 1986, but all for the better—the black tables covered with white linen now have more space between them, and the background music is no longer loud. Yet the high spirits remain. The place draws a mixed crowd of professionals, artists, and local residents who continue to return for the fine food. For starters, try the "naked" shrimp, grilled and spiced with roasted curry paste, mint, and lime juice. Entrées include the luscious Malaysian clams, sautéed with Thai basil and garlic, and the ever-popular boneless Original Tommy Duck with grilled vegetables. *323 Greenwich St. (near Reade St.), tel. 212/334–9190. Reservations advised. Dress: casual chic. AE, DC, MC, V. Closed Sat. lunch and Sun.*

Inexpensive **Bangkok Cuisine.** New York's oldest Thai restaurant is located just north of the Theater District. Some of the specialties include *tod mun pla* (deep-fried fish patties dipped in a sweet sauce), *pad thai* (a peanut-and-noodle dish), and whole fish dinners. *885 Eighth Ave. at 53rd St., tel. 212/581–6370. Reservations advised. Dress: casual. AE, MC, V. No lunch Sun.*

Vietnamese

Expensive **Indochine.** On the ground floor of landmark East Village town houses, the scene here mingles downtown artists with displaced French colonialists. The space is large and airy, decorated with palm leaves and tropical murals. The menu offers exotically spiced Vietnamese and Cambodian specialties. *Rouleau de printemps* (spring roll) is the standard appetizer; stuffed boneless chicken wings or steamed fish in coconut milk make excellent entrees. *430 Lafayette St. between Astor Pl. and E. 4th St., tel. 212/505–5111. Reservations advised. Dress: casual. AE, DC, MC, V. No lunch.*

5 Lodging

by Jane Hershey

A New York–based freelance writer whose work has appeared in Good Housekeeping, US, *and* Elle, *Jane Hershey is a longtime contributor to various Fodor's guides.*

If any single element of your trip to New York City is going to cost you a lot of money, it'll be your hotel bill. Real estate is at a premium here, and labor costs are high, so hoteliers start out with a lot of expenses to cover. And there are enough well-heeled visitors to support competition at the premium end of the spectrum, which is where the profits are. Considering the healthy occupancy rate, market forces are not likely to drive current prices down. We have noted a few budget properties, but on the sliding scale of Manhattan prices even our "Inexpensive" category includes hotels that run as high as $125 for one night's stay in a double room.

Once you've accepted that you must pay the going price, though, you'll have plenty of choices. In general, Manhattan hotels don't measure up to those in other U.S. cities in terms of room size, parking, or outside landscaping. But, this being a sophisticated city, New York hotels usually compensate with fastidious service, sprucely maintained properties, and restaurants that hold their own in a city of very knowledgeable diners.

Basic rules of decorum and dress are observed at the better hotels. With few exceptions, jackets (and frequently ties) are required in formal dining and bar areas after 5 or 6 PM. Bare feet or beach sandals are not allowed, and an overall sloppy appearance won't encourage good service.

Most Manhattan hotels are in the midtown area, so we have categorized them by price range rather than location. Exact prices could be misleading: Properties change their so-called "rack rates" seasonally, and most hotels offer weekend packages that include such tempting extras as complimentary meals, drinks, or tickets to events. Your travel agent may have brochures about such packages; also look for advertisements in travel magazines or the Sunday travel sections of major newspapers such as the *New York Times*, the *Washington Post*, or the *Los Angeles Times*.

Highly recommended lodgings are indicated by a star ★. Though not *every* acceptable hotel has been included, enough ground has been covered to help you find a good match.

Price categories are as follows:

Category	Cost*
Very Expensive	over $260
Expensive	$180–$260
Moderate	$130–$180
Inexpensive	under $125

**All prices are for a standard double room, excluding 18¼% city and state sales tax and $2 occupancy tax.*

The following credit card abbreviations are used: AE, American Express; DC, Diners Club; MC, MasterCard; V, Visa.

Very Expensive

★ **The Carlyle.** Located in one of the city's finest residential areas, this beautifully appointed traditional hotel is considered one of New York's finest. The mood is English manor house; larger rooms and suites, many of them decorated by the famous interior designer Mark Hampton, have terraces, pantries, and antique furnishings. Baths, though more subdued than others in town, are marbled and chock-full of de rigueur amenities such as hair dryers, fine toiletries, and makeup mirrors. Most visitors have heard about the famous Café Carlyle, where performers such as Bobby Short entertain. But the hotel also contains the charming Bemelman's Bar, with whimsical animal murals on the walls and live piano music at night, and the formal Carlyle Restaurant, with French cuisine and old-fashioned courtly service. *35 E. 76th St. at Madison Ave., 10021, tel. 212/744–1600. 185 rooms. Facilities: restaurant, café, bar, lounge, fitness center, VCRs and stereos, fax machines, kitchenettes and pantries in larger units, meeting rooms. AE, DC, MC, V.*

★ **The Mark.** Just one block north of the Carlyle, the former Madison Avenue Hotel has recently been completely redone by its new owner, Rafael Hotels. Even the least expensive rooms have

Aberdeen, **28**
Algonquin, **22**
Beekman Tower, **13**
Best Western Woodward, **10**
Carlyle, **3**
Chatwal Inn, **21**
Chatwal Inn on Park, **29**
Dumont Plaza, **26**
Holiday Inn Crowne Plaza, **16**
Hotel Edison, **19**
Journey's End, **24**
Loew's New York, **11**
Mark, **2**
N.Y. Int'l Youth Hostel, **1**
Pierre, **7**
The Plaza, **8**
President Hotel, **18**
Quality Inn, **20**
Radisson Empire Hotel, **6**
Ramada Inn, **17**
Roger Smith Winthrop, **15**
Royalton, **23**
Shelburne , **25**
Sloane House YMCA, **27**
Southgate Tower, **30**
Surrey Hotel, **4**
Vanderbilt YMCA, **14**
Waldorf-Astoria, **12**
West Side YMCA, **5**
Wyndham, **9**

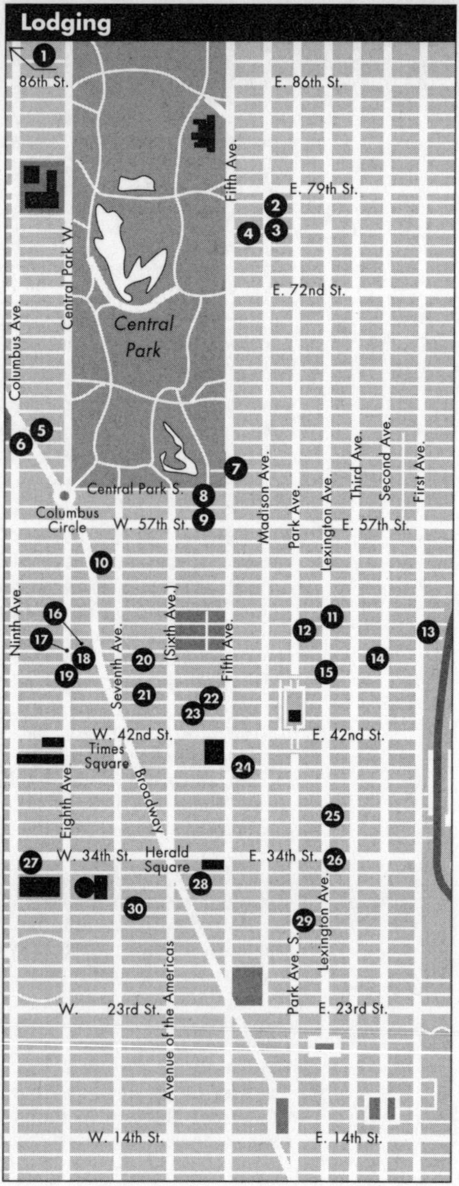

high-quality TVs and VCRs, and its bathrooms feature Art Deco tiles or marble, deep tubs, *and* separate stall showers. Most rooms have pantries, too. Color schemes are warm to reflect the neoclassical Italian motif. There is an elegant restaurant and lounge called Mark's, which features the cuisine of chef Philippe Boulot. The staff seems committed and professional. *25 E. 77th St., 10021, tel. 212/744–4300 or 800/THE–MARK. 185 rooms. Facilities: restaurant, café, lounge, meeting rooms, VIP suites with terraces. AE, DC, MC, V.*

★ **The Pierre.** One might expect haughtiness along with the creamy, oriental-carpeted halls and bright chandeliers, but you won't find that here: The staff has a sense of fun about working in these posh surroundings. Rooms, most of which have been recently refurbished, are traditionally decorated in soft florals with quilted bedspreads. Bathrooms have recently been upgraded and are generously stocked with Four Seasons' amenities. Café Pierre can hold its own against many of the city's best spots; the Bar features low-key jazz piano in the evenings, and formal afternoon tea is served under the blue cherubim-filled dome of the Rotunda. *5th Ave. at 61st St., 10021, tel. 212/838–8000 or 800/332–3442. 204 rooms. Facilities: restaurant, bar, tearoom, meeting rooms, manned elevators, packing service upon request, hand-laundry service. AE, DC, MC, V.*

The Plaza. When real-estate developer and casino operator Donald Trump purchased this National Historic Landmark in 1988, locals shuddered a bit but so far, misgivings have been unfounded. This former haunt of F. Scott Fitzgerald, George M. Cohan, Frank Lloyd Wright, and the Beatles is ready to receive a relatively demanding public. New color schemes are in burgundy or teal blue; fresh, floral-patterned quilted spreads grace the large beds. Furnishings, though still "hotel-like" in most units, are of high quality. Bathrooms, even those not yet fully redone, have fluffy new towels and French toiletries. One real advantage here is the size of guest rooms—only a handful of other classic properties can offer similar spaciousness in nearly all accommodations. Food-and-beverage service has made major strides, and current executive chef Kerry Simon (formerly of Lafayette and Lutèce) will certainly earn plaudits here. The last word was that Trader Vic's bar—renowned for its elaborate exotic drinks—will stay open, although the space formerly occupied by its restaurant might be converted into a health club. *5th Ave. at 59th St., 10019, tel. 212/759–3000 or 800/228–3000. 807 rooms. Facilities: 2 restaurants, 2 bars, café, art gallery, handicapped-guest rooms, meeting rooms, packing service upon request, large concierge staff. AE, DC, MC, V.*

Expensive

Holiday Inn Crowne Plaza. The new deluxe flagship of the famous commercial hotel chain has been built on the exact site of the original music publishing company of Irving Berlin, who wrote the music for the movie *Holiday Inn*, from which the chain took its name. The opulent public areas are decorated in soft beige and rose tones. Upstairs, the decent-size rooms pick up the rose color scheme, this time adding a touch of teal blue. Guest rooms begin at the 16th floor, so that everyone gets a fine view from the panoramic windows. Bathrooms are beyond basic, though the amenities found within could be more lavish. Another minor drawback is the serious lack of closet space, even in the suites. There is a large restaurant, The Broadway Grill. *Broadway at 49th St., tel. 212/977–4000 or 800/HOLIDAY. 770 rooms. Facilities: 3 restaurants, café, lounge, fitness center, pool, ballroom, meeting rooms, business center. AE, DC, MC, V.*

The Royalton. Former Studio 54 disco kings Ian Schrager and the late Steve Rubell, in their quest for a second career as New York hotel moguls, completely rehabilitated this once-shabby property directly across from the Algonquin (*see* below). The Royalton, with its witty "art moderne" design by French decorator Philippe Starck, has a plush but slightly spooky atmosphere: The halls are narrow and dark, as are some of the strangely shaped rooms. Still, the beds and other furnishings are quite comfy, and the bathrooms are decidedly fun—they all have either oversize slate shower stalls or giant circular tubs (a few have both). Toiletries are elegant, and so is the service. The restaurant, Restaurant 44, has finally been granted a liquor license, and it's worth noting that this is the only place on hotel premises where guests can purchase liquor. *44 W. 44th St., 10036, tel. 212/869-4400 or 800/635-9013. 205 rooms. Facilities: restaurant with bar, meeting rooms, game and library areas, VCRs, stereos. AE, DC, MC, V.*

The Waldorf-Astoria. Along with the Plaza (*see* above), this Art Deco masterpiece personifies New York at its most lavish and powerful. Hilton, its owner, has spent a fortune on refurbishing both public areas and guest rooms. Original murals and mosaics, elaborate plaster ornamentation, fine old-wood walls and doors—all look fresh and new. In the guest rooms, some of which start at the low end of this category, there are new bedspreads, carpets, and other signs of upgrading. Bathrooms throughout are old but beautifully kept up and rather spacious by today's standards. There has been a move to modernize the menu at Peacock Alley, where Waldorf salad first made news. Service in the dining areas, however, can be pokey and rude, especially outside of regular mealtimes. The hotel's richly tinted, hushed lobby serves as an interior centerpoint of city life; it's nice to see the rest of the place looking proud, too. *301 Park Ave., 10022, tel. 212/355-3000 or 800/HILTONS. 1,692 rooms. Facilities: 3 restaurants, coffee shop, tearoom, lounge, ballroom, meeting rooms. AE, DC, MC, V.*

Moderate

★ **The Algonquin.** While this landmark property's English-drawing-room atmosphere and burnished-wood lobby are being kept intact, its working parts (the plumbing, for instance) are being improved under new Japanese owners. Management is also redecorating, restoring the old mahogany doors and trim, improving the telephone service, and creating a conference and business area. This much-beloved hotel, where the Round Table group of writers and wits once met for lunch, still shelters many a celebrity, particularly literary types visiting nearby publishing houses or the *New Yorker* magazine offices across the street. Bathrooms and sleeping quarters retain Victorian-style fixtures and furnishings, only now there are larger, firmer beds, modern TVs, VCRs (upon request), computerized phones, and Caswell-Massey toiletries. Personal service, especially for repeat customers, continues to be excellent. *59 W. 44th St., 10036, tel. 212/840–6800 or 800/548–0345. 165 rooms. Facilities: restaurant, 2 lounges, meeting rooms, complimentary parking on weekends, business center. AE, DC, MC, V.*

Journey's End. This Canadian chain's first Manhattan property is what the demanding bargain hunter has been waiting for. No-nonsense, clean, attractive rooms and baths are at one fixed price. Most accommodations come with queen-size beds; all have modern TVs and telephones with long cords. Guests can use a small lounge area for complimentary coffee and newspapers. There were plans at press time for an independently owned Italian restaurant to open on the premises. At night, this part of Midtown is somewhat quiet and therefore prone to street crime. However, security at the hotel appears to be superior. Another plus—it's just a few blocks away from the airport bus departure area on Park Avenue near Grand Central Terminal. *3 E. 40th St., 10016, tel. 212/447–1500 or 800/668–4200. 189 rooms. Facilities: lounge, restaurant, business services on request. AE, DC, MC, V.*

Loew's New York Hotel. Loews' moderate-price New York property has an impersonal style, but most of its regulars—business travelers—don't mind because the hotel generally runs quite well. Rooms, most of them recently refurbished, are standard fare. The new Lexington Avenue Grill is a vast improvement over Maude's, as is the striking new maroon art deco carpeting and wood-tone lobby. Loews takes care of its properties, so the Summit can more than hold its own with some of its neighbors. *Lexington Ave. at 51st St., 10022, tel. 212/752–7000. 766 rooms. Facilities: restaurant, lounge, meeting rooms, fitness center. AE, DC, MC, V.*

★ **Manhattan Suites East.** Here's a group of good-value properties for the traveler who likes to combine full hotel service with independent pied-à-terre living. These nine midtown hotels have different characters and varying prices, though all fall within the Moderate category. The four best are the recently redone **Beekman Tower** (3 Mitchell Pl.), near the United Nations and on the edge of a trendy East Side residential area; the **Dumont Plaza** (150 E. 34th St.), especially convenient for convention goers with its location on a direct bus line to the Javits Center; the **Surrey Hotel** (20 E. 76th St.), in the neighborhood of Madison Avenue art galleries and designer boutiques; and the **Southgate Tower** (371 7th Ave.), the most attractive and secure place to sleep within close range of Madison Square Garden and Penn Station. Except for the modern style at the Dumont, all have traditional guest-room decor; the Surrey's rooms border on the truly elegant. Most accommodations have pantries, and larger units have dining areas with full-size tables. The Beekman, Surrey, Shelburne, and Dumont Plaza have restaurants and room service. The Dumont, Southgate, and Shelburne have on-premises fitness centers. Other hotels in this group tend to be more residential, except for the full-service **Shelburne** (303 Lexington Ave.); many top corporations use them as interim lodgings for newly relocated executives. The older hotels in the group do have some disappointing rooms, but overall these properties are outstanding for the price, considering their convenience, location, and space. Their weekend package rates are hard to beat. *Sales office, 505 E. 75th St., 10001, tel. 212/772-2900 or 800/ME-SUITE. AE, DC, MC, V.*

Radisson Empire Hotel. This old hotel recently changed ownership, so it's a matter of time before one knows what's what, but since the new owner is media mogul John Kluge, the Empire should only gain in luster. The lobby is warm and inviting; halls are decorated in soft gray with elegant lamps. Rooms and suites are a bit like small boxes, but nicely furnished; bathrooms are immaculate if on the small side. The restaurant is new, and the neighborhood is loaded with all-hours dining options. For the money, you'll be hard-pressed to find a cleaner, more conveniently located hotel. *Broadway at 63rd St., 10023, tel. 212/265-7400, 800/221-6509, or 800/223-9868. 368 rooms. Facilities: restaurant, coffee shop. AE, DC, MC, V.*

The Roger Smith Winthrop. Don't be put off by the dusty, faded lobby—the hotel is in the process of a gradual redecoration. Lobby and public areas have been remodeled. The guest rooms upstairs are clean, well decorated, and spacious, and special units have small but luxurious marble baths with Jacuzzis. All rooms have pantries, and there's a complimentary Continental breakfast. A dingy coffee shop downstairs was recently turned into a full restaurant and a tea lounge. *501 Lexington Ave., 10017, tel. 212/755-1400 or 800/241-3848. 200 rooms. Facilities: restaurant, meeting room. AE, DC, MC, V.*

The Wyndham. This genteel treasure sits across from The Plaza and adjacent to the Helmsley Park Lane. The savvy, independent traveler who cares more about gracious rooms and a friendly atmosphere than about imposing lobbies and hand-to-mouth service might well choose this spot over its neighbors. Owner and general manager John Mados keeps prices down by not offering room service or fancy amenities; what he does provide is some of the prettiest and most spacious accommodations in Manhattan. Even the least expensive double room has fresh floral-print bedspreads, comfortable chairs, and decorator wall coverings. A slight drawback is the old-fashioned, white-tile bathrooms. Suites (all of which come with pantries) start as low as $160 per night; they are painted in sunny shades and fitted with antique furniture, tasteful Chinese rugs, and an eclectic mix of everything else. The small lobby is unusually secure—a doorman controls the "in" buzzer 24 hours a day. This hotel is a favorite of stars such as Carol Burnett and media personalities Leonard Maltin and Barbara Walters. *42 W. 58th St., 10019, tel. 212/753-3500. 201 rooms. Facilities: restaurant. AE, DC, MC, V.*

Inexpensive

★ **Chatwal Inns.** The six Chatwal properties, located mostly in the Broadway midtown area, provide clean, attractively designed rooms at reasonable prices. Don't be put off by the rather dingy facades of some of the hotels—rooms at all six locations are immaculate and, though somewhat small, have all the basic amenities travelers have come to expect, including bathroom toiletries, telephones, and TVs. All guests receive a complimentary continental breakfast and some of the larger properties have on-premises full-service restaurants as well. *Aberdeen (17 W. 32nd), Chatwal Inn (132 W. 45th), Chatwal Inn on Park (429 Park Ave. S.), President Hotel (234 W. 48th), Best Western Woodward (210 W. 55th), and Quality Inn (157 W. 47th); Tel. 800/826–4667, or 800/621–4667 in Canada. Facilities: restaurants, small meeting rooms, lounges, depending on the property. AE, DC, MC, V.*

Hotel Edison. A popular budget stop for tour groups from here and abroad, this offbeat old hotel is getting a face-lift. A gruesome murder scene for *The Godfather* was shot in what is now Sophia's restaurant, and the pink plaster coffee shop has become a hot place to eavesdrop on show-business gossip thanks to such celebrity regulars as Jackie Mason. Guest rooms are brighter and fresher than the dark corridors seem to hint. There's no room service, but this part of the theater district has so many restaurants and delis that it doesn't matter much. *228 W. 47th St., 10036, tel. 212/840–5000. 1,000 rooms. Facilities: restaurant, coffee shop, bar. AE, DC, MC, V.*

New York International Youth Hostel. American Youth Hostels recently opened this ambitious facility on Manhattan's Upper West Side. Here, in a renovated 19th-century Gothic-style building, you'll find dormitory accommodations at rock-bottom prices. In addition, the hostel provides conference areas, kitchens, and dining rooms. There are no private baths; rooms hold up to six beds; and guests can rent sheets. All ages are welcome, but there is a limit of one week per stay. Although the immediate neighborhood is still a bit rough, the location is convenient to Columbia University, Harlem, and new stores and eating spots on upper Broadway and Columbus and Amsterdam avenues. This is a welcome alternative for the self-sufficient traveler. At press time, the hostel was going through an early shakedown period, so call in advance about exact prices and available amenities. *891 Amsterdam Ave., 10025, tel. 212/932–*

2300. 90 rooms. Facilities: dining area, patio, kitchen, self-service laundry, travel service desk, conference rooms for nonprofit groups. AE, DC, MC, V.

Ramada Inn. Another of Loews' budget properties, this motel-style building has an outdoor rooftop swimming pool and lounge area with snack bar. Rooms and suites were recently upgraded. Daily garage rates are reasonable. This is a good bet for theater-bound families during the summer months. *48th St. at 8th Ave., 10019, tel. 212/581–7000 or 800/2–RAMADA. 366 rooms. Facilities: restaurant, lounge, pool, meeting room. AE, DC, MC, V.*

Vanderbilt YMCA. Of the various Manhattan Ys offering accommodations, this is the best as far as location and facilities are concerned. Although rooms hold up to four people, they are little more than dormitory-style cells—even with only one or two beds to a room, you may feel crowded. Each room does have a late-model TV, however. There are no private baths; communal showers and toilets are clean. Guests are provided with basics such as towels and soap. Besides the low price, this Y offers instant free membership to its on-premises pool, gym, running track, exercise rooms, and sauna. Many of the athletic and public areas, including the pool, have been remodeled. An informal cafeteria and a friendly hospitality desk encourage travelers to mix with one another. The Turtle Bay neighborhood is safe, convenient, and interesting (the United Nations is a few short blocks away). Other YMCAs in town include the 561–room **West Side Y** (5 W. 63rd St., 10023, tel. 212/787–4400), which may be hard to get into but is in the desirable Lincoln Center area; and the 1,490–room **Sloane House YMCA** (356 W. 34th St., 10001, tel. 212/760–5860), which is in a gritty and somewhat unsafe neighborhood. *224 E. 47th St., 10017, tel. 212/755–2410. 430 rooms. Facilities: cafeteria, meeting rooms, self-service laundry, gift shop, luggage storage, pool, fitness center. No credit cards.*

Bed-and-Breakfasts

Hundreds of rooms are available on a bed-and-breakfast basis in Manhattan and the outer boroughs, principally Brooklyn. B&Bs almost always cost well below $100 a night; some singles are available for under $50.

New York B&Bs, however, are not the quaint old mansions you find in other localities. They fall into two categories: (1) *Hosted apartments*, a bedroom in an apartment where the host is present; (2) *unhosted apartments*, entire apartments that are temporarily vacant. The unhosted option is scarcer and somewhat more expensive.

Along with saving money, B&Bs permit you to mingle with New Yorkers and stay in "real" neighborhoods rather than in tourist enclaves. The disadvantages are that accommodations, amenities, service, and privacy fall far short of what you get in hotels. Sometimes you really do get breakfast and sometimes you don't. And you usually can't pay by credit card.

Here are a few reservation agencies that book B&B accommodations in and near Manhattan. There is no fee for the service, but they advise you to make reservations as far in advance as possible. It's a good idea to find out something about the city before you contact them, and then to request accommodations in a neighborhood that you prefer.

Bed and Breakfast Network of New York (134 W. 32nd St., Suite 602, 10001, tel. 212/645–8134).
City Lights Bed and Breakfast, Ltd. (Box 20355, Cherokee Station, 10028, tel. 212/737–7049).
New World Bed and Breakfast (150 5th Ave., Suite 711, 10011, tel. 212/675–5600 or 800/443–3800).
Urban Ventures (306 W. 38th St., 10018, tel. 212/594–5650).

6 The Arts and Nightlife

The Arts

Full schedules of weekly entertainment and cultural events appear in *New York* magazine's "Cue" listings; they include capsule summaries of Broadway, Off-Broadway, and Off-Off-Broadway shows and concerts, performance times, and ticket prices. The Arts & Leisure section of the Sunday *New York Times* lists and describes events but provides no service information. The Theater Directory in the daily *New York Times* advertises ticket information for Broadway and Off-Broadway shows. Listings of arts events appear weekly in *The New Yorker* and *Village Voice*.

Theater

New York theater is the benchmark for quality and variety. At the height of the season, theatergoers might see anything from full-scale star-studded Broadway musicals to intimate, locally developed dramas at nearly 40 Broadway theaters, 50 Off-Broadway theaters, and 200 Off-Off-Broadway houses. Generally, Broadway productions are the most extravagant and expensive, while the more daring, if less polished, shows are found Off and Off-Off Broadway. Production costs aside, provocative theater can be found anywhere in this city.

Broadway theaters are located in the Theater District, most of which lies between Broadway and Eighth Avenue, from 43rd to 52nd streets. Some of these theaters are small gems, comfortable and luxurious yet intimate enough to make the audience feel part of the show. The newer, larger theaters are no less luxurious. All performers work under an Actors Equity contract that guarantees them a basic minimum salary. Ticket prices range from $22.50 to as much as $100, depending on the show, the time of performance, and the location of the seat. Generally, plays are less expensive than musicals; and matinees (Wednesday, Saturday, and sometimes Sunday) and weeknight performances cost less than shows on Friday and Saturday nights. Most Broadway theaters are "dark" (closed) on Monday, although some are dark on other days.

Off-Broadway theater has professional performers but generally less elaborate productions. The theaters are located all over town. Many can be found along Theater Row, a strip of 42nd Street between Ninth and Tenth avenues; others are located in Greenwich Village, and some are on the Upper West Side. Ticket prices range from $15 to $75, with most falling into the $20–$25 range.

Off-Off-Broadway theater is alternative theater. Performers and production staff may be professionals, but they get little or no salary. Although you won't find lavish sets and plush seating, plays can be highly professional—with performances of everything from Shakespeare to mixed-media performance art. Off-Off-Broadway houses are located in all kinds of spaces—lofts, church basements, converted storefronts—all over town. Tickets rarely exceed $15, and you can phone ahead for reservations. The *Village Voice* contains the most comprehensive Off-Off-Broadway listings.

It's easy to buy tickets for Broadway and Off-Broadway shows; you can do it even before you reach New York. All Broadway show tickets are available by phone from either **Tele-Charge** (tel. 212/239–6200) or **Ticketron** (tel. 212/246–0102). You pay the price of the tickets plus a surcharge to a major credit card and pick them up at the box office before the show. Both of these services operate 24 hours a day, seven days a week. Similar arrangements are available for Off-Broadway through **HIT–TIX** (tel. 212/564–8038), **Ticketmaster** (tel. 212/307–7171), or individual theaters.

In New York, you can buy Broadway tickets at the box offices, which are open most of the day and evening. Tickets for many Off-Broadway shows are available at **Ticket Central** (416 W. 42nd St., tel. 212/279–4200). Tickets for the hottest shows in town—of late *The Phantom of the Opera* and *Six Degrees of Separation*—may be available only through ticket brokers. Brokers in New York can sell the ticket for full price plus a *legal* commission of $2 per ticket and sometimes additional service charges; consequently, many operate out of New Jersey, where such limits don't apply. Look them up in the Manhattan Yellow Pages under "Ticket Sales—Entertainment & Sports."

For discounts of nearly 50% on Broadway and Off-Broadway shows, you can try your luck at **TKTS** (tel. 212/354-5800). This nonprofit service sells day-of-performance tickets for half the regular price, plus a $2 surcharge per ticket. Supply is erratic. Sometimes it seems that every show in town appears on the display board just outside the ticket window. At other times only long-runing hits and little-known sleepers are available.

The main TKTS booth is located in the Theater District on Duffy Square, a triangle formed by Broadway, Seventh Avenue, and 47th Street. It's open from 3 to 8 PM daily for evening performances, 10 to 2 for Wednesday and Saturday matinees, and noon to 8 for Sunday matinee and evening performances. A TKTS booth at 2 World Trade Center opens earlier in the day and generally has shorter lines. Its hours are weekdays from 11 to 5:30, Saturday from 11 to 1. Matinee and Sunday tickets are sold the day before the performance; Off-Broadway tickets are sold 11 AM to 1 PM for evening performances only. Another TKTS booth in front of Borough Hall in Brooklyn (tel. 718/625-5015) operates Tuesday–Friday 11–5:30 and Saturday 11–3:30 for evening performances only. Matinee and Sunday tickets are available the day before the performance; Off-Broadway tickets are sold only until 1 PM. TKTS accepts only cash or traveler's checks—no checks or credit cards.

The Duffy Square lines are long but congenial, with street entertainers galore and envoys from some of the shows trying to lure you out of line with no-wait discounts. It may be worth a trip to the World Trade Center or Brooklyn TKTS so you can save the waiting time and plan the remainder of the afternoon around your evening at the theater.

Concerts

Much of New York's serious music scene clusters around the magnificent concert halls and theaters of Lincoln Center (Broadway and 65th St., tel. 212/877–2011). **Avery Fisher Hall** (tel. 212/874–2424) is the home of the New York Philharmonic Orchestra, the American Philharmonic, the Mostly Mozart festival, and visiting orchestras and soloists. Smaller **Alice Tully Hall** (tel. 212/362–1911), in the Juilliard School of Music building, features chamber music and jazz performances. Although most tickets are sold on a subscription basis, individual seats may be available at the box office in advance or through Centercharge (tel. 212/874–6770).

Since 1891, playing **Carnegie Hall** (W. 57th St. at 7th Ave., tel. 212/247–7800) has epitomized a musician's ascent to the big time. Now it presents visiting orchestras, recitals, chamber music, and pop concerts. The **Weill Recital Hall** features lesser-known artists at lower prices. Student/senior rush tickets are available from 6 PM on performance nights. Public tours are given on Tuesday and Thursday; call 212/247–7800 for information.

Merkin Concert Hall (129 W. 67th St., tel. 212/362–8719) features classical chamber music. Though threatened with gentrification-motivated demolition, **Symphony Space** (2537 Broadway at 95th St., tel. 212/864–5400) continues to present an eclectic program of concerts, literary readings, dance, and drama at painless (free–$35) prices. The **Metropolitan Museum of Art** (1000 Fifth Ave., tel. 212/570–3949) hosts a concert series in its 708-seat Grace Rainey Rogers auditorium. The **92nd Street Y** (1395 Lexington Ave., tel. 212/996–1100) offers chamber music and recitals by top-name musicians.

Concerts are also performed regularly at churches, colleges, museums, recital halls, lofts, parks, and other spaces throughout the city. To find out when and where, consult the Music and Dance section of *New York* magazine, the Sunday *New York Times* Arts & Leisure section, or listings in the *New Yorker*.

A TKTS-like operation called **Bryant Park Music and Dance Discount Ticket Booth** sells discount day-of-performance tickets for music and dance concerts all over the city—including Lincoln Center and Carnegie Hall. Tickets cost half the regular price plus a $2 service charge. *42nd*

St. just east of Sixth Ave., tel. 212/382–2323. Open Tues., Thurs., Fri., noon–2, 3–7; Wed. & Sat. 11–2, 3–7; Sun. noon–6. Cash or traveler's checks only.

Opera

The **Metropolitan Opera** (Broadway at 65th St., tel. 212/362–6000), at Lincoln Center, is a sublime setting for mostly classic operas performed by world-class stars. Tickets can be expensive—up to $115—and hard to get, but low-price standing-room tickets may be available.

New York City Opera (Broadway at 65th St., tel. 212/870–5570), at the State Theater, Lincoln Center, is a first-class opera company with lower ticket prices—under $50—and an innovative and unpredictable schedule.

Other New York opera companies include the **Amato Opera Theatre** (319 Bowery, tel. 212/228–8200), a downtown showcase for young performers. **New York Gilbert and Sullivan Players** (251 W. 91st St., Apt. 4C, tel. 212/769–1000) perform G & S classics Christmas and other times, **Opera Ebony** (2109 Broadway, Suite 1418, tel. 212/874–7245) is an all black company performing major and minor classics, and at **Repertorio Español** (138 E. 27th St., tel. 212/889–2850), performers sing in Spanish. Check *New York* magazine or the *New York Times* for current productions.

Dance

The **American Ballet Theatre** (Broadway at 65th St., tel. 212/362–6000), formerly under the direction of Mikhail Baryshnikov, is the resident company of the Metropolitan Opera House in Lincoln Center. ABT is noted for its lyrical renditions of story ballets during the spring (April–June) season. Ticket prices start low, around $8 for standing room, and rise to over $60.

The renowned **New York City Ballet** (Broadway at 65th St., tel. 212/870–5570), a resident of Lincoln Center's New York State Theater, reached world-class prominence under the direction of George Balanchine. The largest dance organization in the Western World (107 dancers) performs a spring season in May and June, and a winter program from November through February. Tickets range from $7 to $50.

A Moorish-style former Masonic temple, **City Center** (131 W. 55th St., tel. 212/581–7907) hosts innovative dance companies like the Dance Theater of Harlem, the Paul Taylor Company, and the Joffrey Ballet. The **Joyce Theater** (175 Eighth Ave., tel. 212/242–0800) is an Art Deco former movie house with a contemporary fall and spring season; it is also the New York home of the Feld Ballets/NY. Nearby, the **Dance Theater Workshop** (219 W. 19th St., tel. 212/691–6500) is a second-floor performance space that highlights the work of avant-garde dancers and choreographers. The 127-year-old **Brooklyn Academy of Music** (BAM; 30 Lafayette Ave., Brooklyn, tel. 718/636–4100) features contemporary dance as a component of its Next Wave Festival each fall.

Weekly listings of ballet, modern, and folk dance performances can be found in *New York* magazine and the Arts and Leisure section of the Sunday *New York Times*. Half-price day-of-performance tickets are available at **Bryant Park Music and Dance Discount Ticket Booth** (*see* Concerts, above, for details).

Film

Few cities rival New York's selection of films. Along with all the first-run Hollywood features, an incomparable selection of foreign films, classics, documentaries, and experimental works are playing all over town. The daily *New York Daily News* and *New York Newsday*, the Friday *New York Times*, and the weekly (available Wednesday) *Village Voice* publish schedules and show times for Manhattan movies. *New York* magazine and the *New Yorker* publish programs and capsule reviews but no schedules.

The vast majority of Manhattan theaters are first-run houses. Most charge $7.50 a ticket for adults at all times; some offer off-peak discounts for children and senior citizens. Even though New York has recently lost some of its venerable revival houses (the Thalia, the Regency), many remaining theaters still feature revivals, classics, and off-beat films.

The **Film Forum** (209 W. Houston St., tel. 212/727–8110) in SoHo features contemporary foreign films, documentaries, and other unusual work. **Cinema Village** (22 E. 12th St., tel. 212/505–7320) changes its programs of double-feature revivals three times a week. **Theatre 80 St. Marks** (80 St. Marks Pl., tel. 212/254–7400) in the East Village has different double-feature revival programs nearly every day. The **Public Theater** (425 Lafayette St., tel. 212/598–7171) concentrates on retrospectives and documentaries.

The **American Museum of the Moving Image** (35th Ave. at 36th St., Astoria, tel. 718/784–0077) is found at the historic Kaufman Astoria Studios. The museum presents over 700 programs annually, including major artist-oriented retrospectives, Hollywood classics, experimental videos, and TV documentaries.

The **Museum of Modern Art** (11 W. 53rd St., tel. 212/708–9490) shows film classics every day in two theaters; movies are free with museum admission. The **Collective for Living Cinema** (41 White St., tel. 212/925–3926) in TriBeCa has an ambitious, constantly changing program of experimental films.

Some foreign cultural institutions show films in their respective languages, with subtitles. They include the **Florence Gould Hall** (55 E. 59th St., tel. 212/355–6160), the site for French films sponsored by the French Institute-Alliance Francaise; the German **Goethe House** (1014 Fifth Ave., tel. 212/972–3960); and **Japan Society** (333 E. 47th St., tel. 212/752–3015).

Nightlife

Cabaret

The Ballroom. A Chelsea tapas (Spanish appetizers) bar with top-name cabaret acts and outrageous revues. *253 W. 28th St., tel. 212/244–3005.*

Nightlife Uptown

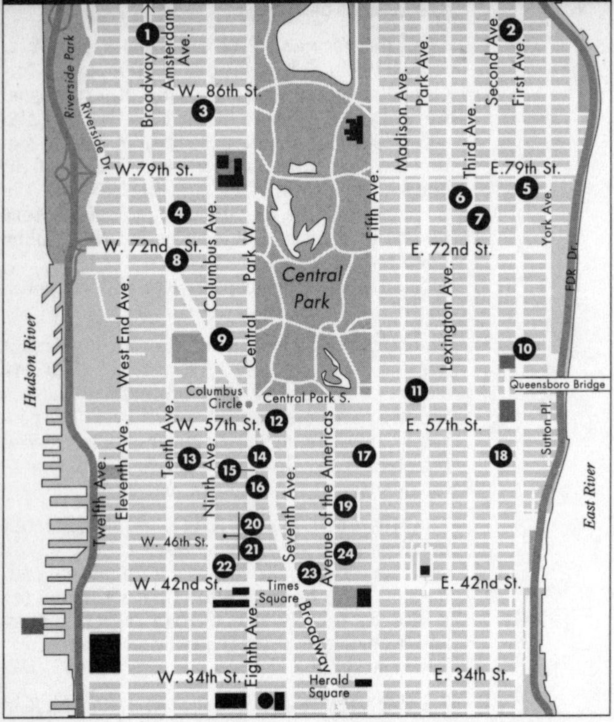

Birdland, **1**
Catch a Rising Star, **5**
Danny's Skylight Room, **21**
Don't Tell Mama, **20**
The Ginger Man, **9**
Hard Rock Cafe, **12**
The Improvisation, **22**
J.G. Melon, **4, 7**
Jan Wallman's, **24**
Jim McMullen's, **6**
Lone Star Roadhouse, **15**
Lucy's Restaurant, **3**
Michael's Pub, **18**
Rainbow Room, **19**
The Red Zone, **13**
Regines, **11**
The Ritz, **14**
Roseland, **16**
Shout!, **23**
Steve McGraw's, **8**
Second Story, **2**
T.G.I. Friday's, **10**
Top of the Sixes, **17**

Nightlife Downtown

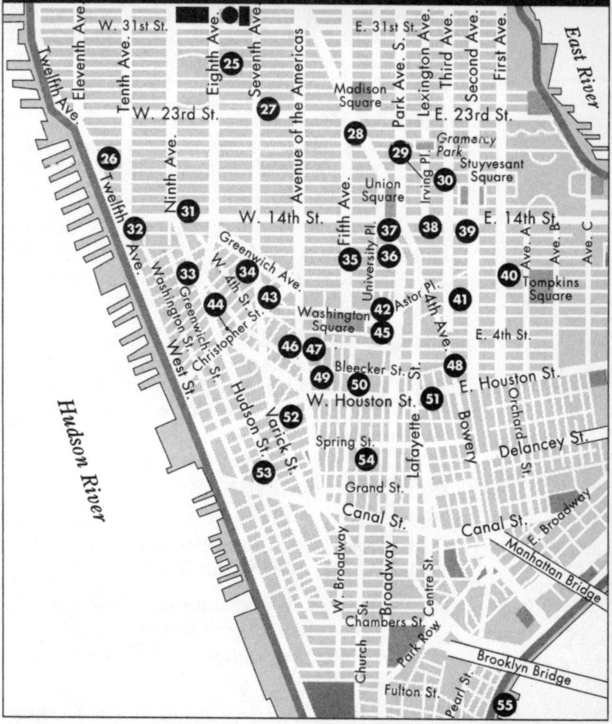

Angry Squire, **27**
The Ballroom, **25**
The Bitter End, **50**
Blue Note, **46**
Bottom Line, **45**
Bradley's, **35**
Café Society, **28**
Cat Club, **37**
CBGB & OMFUG, **48**
Cedar Tavern, **36**
Dan Lynch's Blues Bar, **39**
Downtown Beirut I, **40**
The Duplex, **43**
Eagle Tavern, **31**
Ear Inn, **53**
Eighty-eight's, **44**
Fat Tuesday's, **29**
15 Waverly, **42**
Kilimanjaro, **26**
Knitting Factory, **51**
Mars, **32**
McSorley's Old Ale House, **41**
Palladium, **38**
Pete's Tavern, **30**
S.O.B.'s, **52**
South Street Seaport, **55**
Sweet Basil, **47**
Upstairs at Greene Street, **54**
Village Gate, **49**
Village Vanguard, **34**
White Horse Tavern, **33**

Catch A Rising Star. Continuous comedy and live music by performers on their way up—or down. *1487 First Ave., near 78th St., tel. 212/794–1906. Cover charge: Sun–Thurs. $8; Fri. and Sat. $12. Reservations required.*

Don't Tell Mama. Lively piano bar up front with no cover or minimum and chancey "open mike" policy. Cabaret performers work the back room. *343 W. 46th St., tel. 212/757–0788.*

The Duplex. A bilevel Village club with torch singers and hot comics. *61 Christopher St., tel. 212/255–5438. Shows at 8, 10, and midnight Fri. and Sat.*

Danny's Skylight Room. Danny's is housed in the Grand Sea Palace, a fixture on Restaurant Row. You'll find the entertainment to be a little bit of everything here, from jazz musicians and crooners to pianists and monologuists. *346 W. 46th St., tel. 212/265–8133. Cover charge: $8–$12; depending on entertainment.*

Eighty-eight's. Come to hear the best tunes from Broadway in inventively assembled programs. *228 W. 10th St., tel. 212/924–0088.*

Jan Wallman's. Hot restaurant-cabaret on the ground floor of the Hotel Iroquois features jazz-oriented singers and players. *49 W. 44th St., tel. 212/764–8930.*

The Improvisation. New York's original comedy showcase where all the big-name yucksters (Rodney Dangerfield, Richard Pryor, Robert Klein) earned their first giggles. *358 W. 44th St., tel. 212/765–8268.*

Steve McGraw's. West Side showroom presents scathingly irreverent satirical revues and cabaret shows. *158 W. 72nd St., tel. 212/595–7400.*

Jazz Clubs

Most jazz clubs have substantial cover charges and a drink minimum for table service. You can usually save one or both of these charges by sitting at or standing around the bar.

In Greenwich Village, the **Village Vanguard** (178 Seventh Ave. S, tel. 212/255–4037) is a basement joint that has ridden the crest of every new wave in jazz for over 50 years. The **Village Gate** (Bleecker and Thompson Sts., tel. 212/475-5120) can present different jazz-related acts and shows simultaneously in three places. No cover on the Village Gate terrace. Go to **Sweet Basil** (88 Seventh Ave. S, near Bleecker St., tel. 212/242-1785) for a roomful of jazz memorabilia and top-name groups. The East Village's **Dan Lynch's Blues Bar** (221 Second Ave., tel. 212/677-0911) is full of jazz surprises, especially on Sunday afternoons.

The Blue Note (131 W. Third St., tel. 212/475-8592) is a new incarnation of a legendary jazz club. Smoky and crowded, **Bradley's** (70 University Pl., tel. 212/228-6440) is a low-key place that spotlights piano-and-bass combos. **The Knitting Factory** (47 E. Houston St., tel. 212/219-3055), a hot new place on the frontier of SoHo, features avant-garde groups. **Upstairs at Greene Street** (105 Greene St., tel. 212/925-2415) is a restaurant converted from a three-story parking garage. Greene Street spent a long time looking for its niche, but it seems to have found it with free jazz and an ultracool setting.

Farther uptown, **Angry Squire** (216 Seventh Ave., near 23rd St., tel. 212/242-9066) is a Chelsea neighborhood pub with contemporary sounds from small groups. At cozy **Fat Tuesday's** (190 Third Ave., at 17th St., tel. 212/533-7902), two sets are played every night but Monday in an intimate basement, and there's a popular restaurant/bar upstairs. **Michael's Pub** (211 E. 55th St., tel. 212/758-2272) has mainstream jazz, top vocalists, jazz-based revues—and Woody Allen's Dixieland band most Mondays.

Pop and Rock Clubs

The *Village Voice* carries the best listings of who's playing where on the pop and rock scene.

In Greenwich Village, folk headliners usually dominate the bill at **The Bottom Line** (15 W. Fourth St., off Mercer St., tel. 212/228-6300). Past performers include everyone from Stevie Wonder to Suzanne Vega. For over 25 years **The Bitter End** (147 Bleecker St., tel. 212/673-7030) has been giving a break to folk, rock, jazz, comedy, and country acts. Everyone goes to the **Cat**

Club (76 E. 13th St., tel. 212/505–0090) for dancing. Heavy metal presides, though occasional swing nights vary the tempo. A low-key Irish pub, the **Eagle Tavern** (355 W. 14th St., tel. 212/924–0275) presents traditional Irish music, with bluegrass and comedy thrown in for variety.

CBGB & OMFUG (315 Bowery, tel. 212/982–4052) still blasts eardrums with the hard rock sound of heavy metal.

Farther uptown, dance at **The Ritz** (254 W. 54th St., tel. 212/541–8900), a restored Art Deco ballroom that hosts the newest rock groups. **The Lone Star Roadhouse** (240 W. 52nd St., tel. 212/245–2950) offers big names in country swing and big city blues.

Latin Clubs

15 Waverly (15 Waverly Pl., tel. 212/533–3048). This tropical Village club features Brazilian, Caribbean, and African music. **Kilimanjaro** (531 W. 19th St., tel. 212/627–2333) S.O.B.'s (*see* below) has major competition with this large club, which opened in 1989, riding on the success of the DC original; it features world-beat music. **S.O.B.'s** (Sounds of Brazil) (204 Varick St., tel. 212/243–4940) is a sophisticated tropical setting for south-of-the-border music.

Discos and Dance Clubs

While club-hopping don't miss New York's largest, the **Palladium** (126 E. 14th St., tel. 212/473–7171). Practically an institution by now with Club MTV, it is no longer the hot ticket it was a few years ago, still, this place is to the club scene what Macy's is to shopping. Occupying an old meat-packing warehouse, **Mars** (10th Ave. at 13th St., tel. 212/691–6262) was redone à la early urban decay; take your pick among five levels. The door staff is *very* particular. **The Red Zone** (440 W. 54th St., tel. 212/582–2222), a 14,000-square-foot discotheque, features huge movie screens where images of water-lapped beaches and the Wild West are projected. **Second Story** (415 E. 91st St., tel. 212/410–1360). The East Side coat-and-tie crowd let down their hair (while managing, even in the heat of the moment, to remain impeccably coiffed). Abundant mahogany; rock 'n' roll from the '60s to the '90s.

For "touch dancing" the way they used to do it, 70-year-old **Roseland** (239 W. 52nd St., tel. 212/247-0200) has two orchestras Thursday through Sunday nights and matinees from 2:30 PM. Whoosh through the revolving door at **Café Society** (915 Broadway at 21st St., tel. 212/529-8282) to find soaring ceilings, pink art deco decor, a long, inviting bar, and dinner and dancing. The quixotic entrepreneur who owns Café Society also runs Society Billiards next door. At elegant **Regines** (502 Park Ave. at 59th St., tel. 212/826-0990) an expensive dinner buys access to the disco floor—or you can eat elsewhere and pay a cover charge. Most spectacular of all, the newly remodeled **Rainbow Room** atop the 65-floor RCA Building (30 Rockefeller Center, tel. 212/632-5100) gives you a dance floor straight out of the Hollywood classics.

Bars for Singles (Under 30)

Downtown, there's no dearth of drinking opportunities at **South Street Seaport** (Water and Fulton Sts., tel. 212/732-7678). Bars at this major New York attraction include Roebling's, Jeremy's, the Fulton Street Café, and McDuffy's Irish Coffee House, to name a few. On warm Friday evenings the Seaport takes on the appearance of an Ivy League homecoming/college mixer, where Wall street-types raise a glass with young professionals from around the city. The **Ear Inn** (326 Spring St., near Greenwich St., tel. 212/226-9060) boasts an archetypal juke box and regular poetry readings. Young people throng to **McSorley's Old Ale House** (15 E. 7th St., tel. 212/473-9148), one of the oldest and most crowded bars in the city. **Downtown Beirut I** (158 First Ave., tel. 212/777-9011) is an offbeat East Village hangout that attracts artists and student types.

Farther uptown, lines are usually waiting outside the **Hard Rock Café** (221 W. 57th St., tel. 212/459-9320), a shrine to rock 'n' roll. The nine-to-five crowd unwinds to '50s and '60s tunes at **Shout!** (124 W. 43rd St., tel. 212/869-2088). On the Upper East Side, **T.G.I. Friday's** (1152 First

Ave. at 63rd St., tel. 212/832–8512) has a long tradition as a congenial gathering place. On the Upper West Side, young crowds congregate at **Lucy's Restaurant** (503 Columbus Ave., tel. 212/787–3009).

Clubs and Bars for Singles (Over 30)

Three traditional Greenwich Village literary hangouts continue to attract local regulars and curious visitors. **Pete's Tavern** (129 E. 18th St., tel. 212/473–7676), a crowded, friendly saloon, is famous as the place where O. Henry wrote "The Gift of the Magi." The **White Horse Tavern** (567 Hudson St. at 11th St., tel. 212/243–9260), which figures prominently in the legend and lore of Dylan Thomas, now has outdoor seating during summer. The **Cedar Tavern** (82 University Pl., tel. 212/243–9355) was a haunt of beatnik writers and abstract expressionist painters.

Farther uptown, **Jim McMullen's** (1341 Third Ave., tel. 212/861–4700) is a young, upscale, Upper East Side watering hole with a large, busy bar decked with bouquets of fresh flowers. The **Ginger Man** (51 W. 64th St., tel. 212/399–2358) is a reliable Lincoln Center area establishment which offers a seemingly endless warren of rooms, handsome Tiffany lamps, and famous faces from nearby ABC–TV. On the 39th floor of 666 Fifth Avenue, **Top of the Sixes** (tel. 212/757–6662) offers 360-degree views to a large cocktail-hour crowd. East Side, West Side, the **J. G. Melon** establishments (1291 Third Ave. at 74th St., tel. 212/744–0585; and 340 Amsterdam Ave. at 76th St., tel. 212/877–2220) are comfortable, low-pressure places where you can meet people.

Index

Personal Itinerary

Departure *Date*

Time

Transportation

Arrival *Date* *Time*

Departure *Date* *Time*

Transportation

Arrival *Date* *Time*

Departure *Date* *Time*

Transportation

Arrival *Date* *Time*

Departure *Date* *Time*

Transportation

Personal Itinerary

Arrival *Date* *Time*

Departure *Date* *Time*

Transportation

Arrival *Date* *Time*

Departure *Date* *Time*

Transportation

Arrival *Date* *Time*

Departure *Date* *Time*

Transportation

Arrival *Date* *Time*

Departure *Date* *Time*

Transportation

Adresses

Name

Address

Telephone

Name

Address

Telephone

Name

Address

Telephone

Name

Address

Telephone

Name

Address

Telephone

Name

Address

Telephone

Adresses

Name

Address

Telephone

Name

Address

Telephone

Name

Address

Telephone

Name

Address

Telephone

Name

Address

Telephone

Name

Address

Telephone

Fodor's Travel Guides

U.S. Guides

Alaska
Arizona
Boston
California
Cape Cod, Martha's Vineyard, Nantucket
The Carolinas & the Georgia Coast
The Chesapeake Region
Chicago
Colorado
Disney World & the Orlando Area
Florida
Hawaii
Las Vegas, Reno, Tahoe
Los Angeles
Maine,Vermont, New Hampshire
Maui
Miami & the Keys
National Parks of the West
New England
New Mexico
New Orleans
New York City
New York City (Pocket Guide)
Pacific North Coast
Philadelphia & the Pennsylvania Dutch Country
Puerto Rico (Pocket Guide)
The Rockies
San Diego
San Francisco
San Francisco (Pocket Guide)
The South
Santa Fe, Taos, Albuquerque
Seattle & Vancouver
Texas
USA
The U. S. & British Virgin Islands
The Upper Great Lakes Region
Vacations in New York State
Vacations on the Jersey Shore
Virginia & Maryland
Waikiki
Washington, D.C.
Washington, D.C. (Pocket Guide)

Foreign Guides

Acapulco
Amsterdam
Australia
Austria
The Bahamas
The Bahamas (Pocket Guide)
Baja & Mexico's Pacific Coast Resorts
Barbados
Barcelona, Madrid, Seville
Belgium & Luxembourg
Berlin
Bermuda
Brazil
Budapest
Budget Europe
Canada
Canada's Atlantic Provinces
Cancun, Cozumel, Yucatan Peninsula
Caribbean
Central America
China
Czechoslovakia
Eastern Europe
Egypt
Europe
Europe's Great Cities
France
Germany
Great Britain
Greece
The Himalayan Countries
Holland
Hong Kong
India
Ireland
Israel
Italy
Italy 's Great Cities
Jamaica
Japan
Kenya, Tanzania, Seychelles
Korea
London
London (Pocket Guide)
London Companion
Mexico
Mexico City
Montreal & Quebec City
Morocco
New Zealand
Norway
Nova Scotia, New Brunswick, Prince Edward Island
Paris
Paris (Pocket Guide)
Portugal
Rome
Scandinavia
Scandinavian Cities
Scotland
Singapore
South America
South Pacific
Southeast Asia
Soviet Union
Spain
Sweden
Switzerland
Sydney
Thailand
Tokyo
Toronto
Turkey
Vienna & the Danube Valley
Yugoslavia

Wall Street Journal Guides to Business Travel

Europe
International Cities
Pacific Rim
USA & Canada

Special-Interest Guides

Bed & Breakfast and Country Inn Guides:
Mid-Atlantic Region
New England
The South
The West
Cruises and Ports of Call
Healthy Escapes
Fodor's Flashmaps New York
Fodor's Flashmaps Washington, D.C.
Shopping in Europe
Skiing in the USA & Canada
Smart Shopper's Guide to London
Sunday in New York
Touring Europe
Touring USA